Dance with Heaven & Earth

Life Lessons from Zen & Aikido

Anna Sanner

authorHOUSE®

AuthorHouse™ LLC
1663 Liberty Drive
Bloomington, IN 47403
www.authorhouse.com
Phone: 1-800-839-8640

Published by AuthorHouse   10/08/2013

ISBN: 978-1-4772-2088-7 (sc)
ISBN: 978-1-4772-2089-4 (e)

Library of Congress Control Number: 2012910815

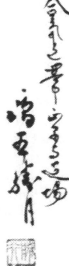

Harmonize with Others
Harmonize with Heaven and Earth
Dance with Others
Dance with Heaven and Earth

Acknowledgements

I would like to thank Itamar Zadoff for supplying materials he collected in his own interviews with Katsuyuki Shimamoto and doing valuable liaison work in Japan while I was not there to take care of things myself, David Gomez for supporting my work with his knowledge, experience, and shared search for aikido solutions to any problem on our path, Paweł Zdunowski, David Kolb, Peter Sager, and Niek Zandee for providing the positive comments on the book's back cover, Ze'ev Erlich and Shmulik Zoltak for their generous motivation and support throughout the project, and all my fellow aikido students at Shosenji Dojo, who made me feel welcome and helped me develop in their midst. Last but not least, I want to thank Shimamoto Shihan's beautiful wife 'Mama-san' for taking care of him, and his son 'Tamayuki-Sensei' for working so hard to support and supplement his father's work.

Contents

Zen Section

Notes for Reading

As there is a differentiation between long and
short 'o' and 'u' sounds in Japanese that leads to
differences in meaning, the long vowel sounds
in Japanese words will be written as 'ō' and 'ū'
respectively. This does not apply to names like
'Shosenji', 'Shoryukai', or 'Osawa', or words like
'dojo' and 'aikido' that are commonly used in
English and have been adopted into the
English language without these
specifications.

The partner or uke practiced with is referred
to as 'he' throughout the book. I have opted for
the masculine pronoun because a) Shimamoto
Shihan mostly demonstrates techniques with
male uke, and the predominant image in my
mind is him talking about them, and b) for
linguistic simplicity and ease of
understanding.

If you are unsure about the meaning of any
Japanese terms you find throughout the book,
please refer to the respective glossary. There is
one glossary for the aikido section and another
for the Zen section that give the corresponding
characters and offer brief explanations for each
term.

静慮振魂の行愛美解脱大乗禅
経行鐘外気不童心お釈迦さん和
教外別伝無心面壁霧困気佛心
放心一末禅警策覚触和不同仏法僧
作務手魂検単以心伝心釈迦坐府
最大乗禅釈尊空心身一如禅
正座定坐禅坐禅会天地投げ禅堂
思惟修自然体能表技思いやり合心
爾今自性如意気の流れ気水の心
内機小乗禅覚触自然体合気

Preface

With a fresh MA in Interpreting and Translating Japanese I moved to Japan in January 2007. I had practiced karate for six years and aikido for about one. After two months in Japan, I discovered Shosenji, a Zen temple with an adjacent aikido dojo in my neighborhood , and met Katsuyuki Shimamoto Shihan, head of both. On February 16th 2007 I attended my first aikido class at Shosenji dojo, the Friday morning women's class. This was the beginning of a long lasting bond with a place that has become like home, a group of people that have become like family, and a teacher who has changed my life.

Although my aikido skills were even more rudimentary at the time than they are now, Shimamoto Shihan's words fascinated me from the beginning, and I never failed to take notes after receiving his instructions. Even though sometimes whole days of work lay between an aikido class and my note taking, what he said tended to remain in my memory with surprising clarity and detail. I consider this the result of his rare skill to convey even the most complex ideas in a simple, coherent, and even entertaining manner that imprinted itself gently and comfortably on my mind and could not possibly be shaken off, just like the touch of his hand when he performed aikido techniques. Shimamoto Shihan exuded integrity. Everything he said and did was an expression of his sincere search for truth and harmony that he offered to share with us.

While explaining the techniques and principles of aikido, Shimamoto Shihan taught me countless useful strategies to approach everyday problems and generally lead a better life - a life in tune with myself, with those around me, and with nature.

I became a devoted student and, serving as his interpreter, began to accompany him on his teaching trips abroad. It was after receiving many enthusiastic words of gratitude from his other foreign followers for being able to understand Shimamoto Shihan's words that I conceived the idea to turn his teachings into a book. Right away, I gathered avid support from among their rows, and to my delight, gained Shimamoto Shihan's approval for the project. Returning from a trip to Poland and the Netherlands in October 2010, I immediately set to work.

After spending many hours writing, editing, arranging and rearranging, translating and discussing my expansive notes on Shimamoto Shihan's teachings with him, the result is now in front of you. I hope his words will inspire you like they have inspired me. May his message of self discipline and harmony cross what O-Sensei Ueshiba called the 'Silver Bridge' and contribute to more peace and harmony in the many minds and regions of this earth. As early as 1961, the founder of aikido visited Hawai'i and expressed his desire to spread the teachings of aikido in the world:

'I wish to build a bridge to bring the different countries of the world together through the harmony and love contained in aikido. I think that aiki, offspring of the martial arts, can unite the people of the world in harmony, in the true spirit of budo, enveloping the world in unchanging love'.

by Anna Sanner, Osaka, August 29th 2011

Katsuyuki Shimamoto

26 Oct 1937	Born in Kita-ku, Osaka City, son of Shosenji Temple's 14th generation Zen priest, 3rd of 5 children
1945	The original Shosenji Temple burned down in WWII
1950-1956	Practiced Okinawan style Shitoryu Karate (2nd dan)
1950-1961	Participated actively in school & university volleyball clubs
1950-1953	Practiced kendo as part of the school curriculum
1956-1960	Enrolled in Buddhist Studies at Komazawa University. Met his future teachers Suzuki Kakuzen and Kisaburo Osawa. Helped found aikido club at Komazawa University; joined and began to practice aikido.
1956-1962	Attended aikido classes at Aikikai Hombu dojo in Tokyo, including classes taught by founder Morihei Ueshiba

1960-1962	Enrolled in Komazawa University Postgraduate Program for Buddhist Studies at the recommendation of Kakuzen Suzuki Sensei
1961	Shosenji Temple moved to Toyonaka City in North Osaka
1962	Head of Shosenji Zen Temple and Shosenji Aikido Dojo
1963-1964	Zen practice at Eiheiji Temple in Fukui Prefecture
1964	Married to Hisako Kawai of Yao, Osaka
1965-1995	Behavioral support/ Social Studies teacher at several junior high schools in Minoo, Osaka
1995	Began traveling abroad to teach aikido: regular visits to the Netherlands, Poland, Australia, Singapore, Canada
2000	Founding of Shoryukai, offshoot of Shosenji Dojo, in Breda, Netherlands headed by Ruud van Ginkel
2008-2010	Chair on the Board of All Japan Aikido Federation
2010	Chair on the Board of Osaka Prefectural Aikido Federation
1 Jan 2010	Awarded 8th dan by Doshu Moriteru Ueshiba

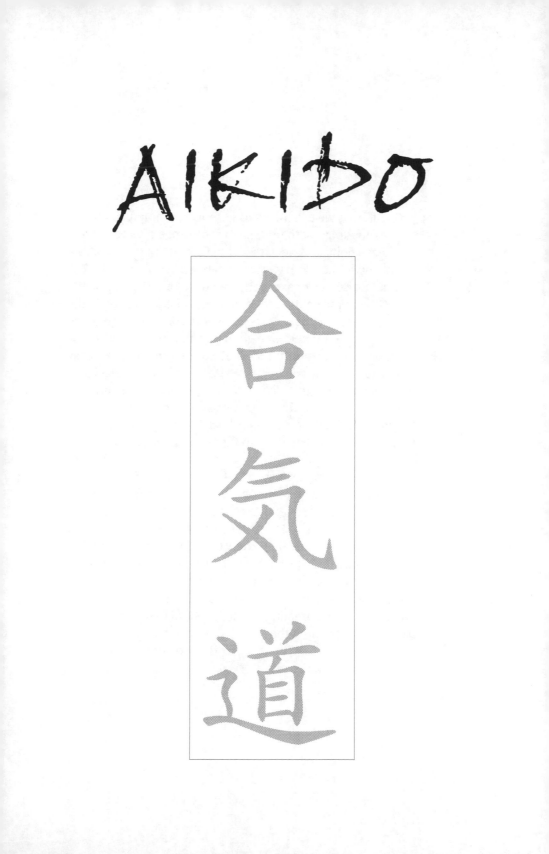

Greetings

Today, we use the word 挨拶 aisatsu simply to refer to a greeting, but to understand the sense of urgency that was originally associated with it, let us take a look at the history of Zen. Zen was once banned in China, and if Zen practitioners were exposed, they were punished by death. Still, some continued to practice their path deep in the mountains. Others were desperate to become Zen practitioners, and went on a dangerous and lonely search, looking for teachers. It was rare that they actually found somebody willing to initiate them into the teachings of Zen. But when they did, this most precious, most unlikely encounter, and the happiness and relief they felt can be described with the character 挨 ai. Nobody was allowed to talk about Zen, so even deep in the mountains, Zen teachings were transmitted silently from heart to heart, from teacher to student. This exchange, the teacher's genuine effort and the student's genuine gratefulness can be described with the character 拶 satsu. Zen teachers and students risked their lives following their path, so imagine how deep the bond was they must have felt when they knew they could trust each other and share their search for truth. Imagine their relief, their deep feelings of friendship, and their gratefulness for each other's presence. This is the sense of urgency we should feel when we offer a greeting to a fellow human being. Offering a heartfelt greeting is the first step we can take to determine the tone of our encounter.

Welcome

To welcome somebody is not simply to sit at home and wait. When you expect a guest, you gently sprinkle water in the entrance hall and get ready to greet him at the gate, or even pick him up at the station. You should not be taken aback when somebody visits. You should be well prepared for the occasion and give your guest an appropriate welcome. This is the same when practicing a technique in aikido. Think of your partner as a guest, and his attack as a visit. Always maintain a mind and posture prepared to welcome your partner - be prepared to welcome anything that might happen to you. Do not discriminate. Welcome.

All - Inclusive

There are people in my dojo who cannot see, people with painful spine diseases, people who have bad legs and cannot walk well. Still, they come to the dojo and practice. They earn their grades like everybody else. They wear hakama. Like everybody else they have to adjust the techniques of aikido to their own bodies. For them, this may be more difficult than for others, but everybody should be given the opportunity to practice at their own pace. Regardless of age, gender, physical condition, background, religion, or nationality, aikido is all-inclusive. True aikido spirit welcomes everybody.

Find A Teacher

I practice calligraphy. Yesterday, I wrote the same character 100 times. When my teacher told me which one was the best, I was surprised because I was not particularly proud of this character. This showed me that my ability to judge calligraphy is not very well developed. It was a good lesson for my ego. Our ego should never become too big. We should not try to judge for ourselves whether our technique is good. As early as we can, we should try to find a teacher who can do this for us. A teacher who can help our true nature emerge, who can polish the material we are made of until it shows its true beauty, who can help us unfold our natural flavor and achieve our full potential.

What is a Teacher?

There is a haiku that expresses an old Japanese teaching:

実るほど
頭を垂れる
稲穂かな

Minoru hodo
Kōbe wo tareru
Inaho kana

As the grain ripens
The rice plant bows down lower
Ready for harvest

A teacher is humble and never treats students disrespectfully. He tries to win against his own weakness, not against others. He is not arrogant. He bows down low and encounters people with respect and humility. Teaching students a set of knowledge or techniques does not make a teacher. A teacher is somebody who is on a desperate quest to find something - answers, forms, techniques, whatever it may be - and shares this quest with his students. As the students see their teacher's desperate search, they learn from it and embark on a genuine search of their own. This is the student - teacher relationship.

Advice for Teachers

Always maintain shizentai. Do not limit your world. Make your field of vision and your scope of action big. Teach the same to your students. When they focus on nothing but one tiny detail, caution them about it. Always check your own attitude. Make sure your scope of perception is wide. Are you focusing on only one student? Are you getting stuck instead of taking things from a different angle? Aikido is simple, but in its simplicity lies its difficulty. Often, students think something is simple and get sloppy about it. Caution them when this happens. Do not let them slack on technical precision. Do not let them get sloppy about their attitude. To achieve this, you must keep checking your own precision and attitude at all times. Make sure you keep searching for shizentai and harmonious interaction. Make sure you keep moving forward on your path. We must not forget these simple, yet most difficult basics of our practice. We need to keep searching for shizentai and for ways to achieve harmony. Our role as teachers is to pass on this genuinely searching mind to our students so they can continue our progress as a whole.

Always Accept

Whatever attack you get, accept it fully. Do not reject it. You can only absorb and control it if you welcome it. As long as you reject an attack it remains outside your sphere of influence, and you have no control over it. If you try to fight and shove your partner it will not work. He will only fight back, and you both get tired, or worse. But if you say 'Yes, thank you!' and invite him into your sphere of influence, he will agree with you and fall of his own accord. This is what we do in aikido. Whatever we get, we always accept.

Your Partner is Your Guest 1 - 打ち水 Uchi-Mizu

In Japan, we have a tradition called 打ち水 uchi-mizu: we sprinkle water in the entrance hall when we expect a visitor. In the tea ceremony and at Zen temples, this is considered the first service rendered to the guest. Rather than dumping out a whole bucket, the water is sprinkled evenly with the finger tips. It cannot be done immediately before the guest arrives, or the floor will be slippery. Neither can it be done too long before he arrives, because it will get dusty again. In aikido, think of your partner as a dear guest honoring you with a visit. When he arrives, you should be ready. You should have sprinkled water in the entrance hall just a little while ago. Everything should be prepared. Keep an open, welcoming posture. When your guest arrives, invite him in exactly the way you want to receive him. Make it easy and pleasant for him to enter.

Your Partner is Your Guest 2 – A Pleasant Exchange

When your guest has followed you into the house, you have a good time together. In aikido, this corresponds with the middle part of the technique. Both you and your partner should enjoy this exchange. Being the host, it is your task to create a pleasant, harmonious setting for you and your partner to converse in. When inviting your partner into your sphere, focus your efforts on inviting and sustaining a sincere, fruitful and harmonious conversation. Communicate from the heart. Every technique should be a pleasant exchange.

Your Partner is Your Guest 3 – 残心 Zanshin and 放心 Hōshin

After you have enjoyed a pleasant exchange with your guest, accompany him to the gate and say good bye. Watch him until he is out of sight. When he has turned the corner or walked too far away for you to see him, bow and send a sincere prayer: 'Thank you for coming. Have a safe trip home.' Only then, turn your mind towards other activities. This is Japanese etiquette.

In aikido this translates into a concept called 残心 zanshin (remaining mind). The technique is not yet complete after the middle part. Only for a moment, keep your mind, heart, and center directed towards your partner and send a short, sincere prayer: 'Thank you. Safe trip.' This is zanshin.

A concept as important as zanshin, the proverbial other side of the coin, is 放心 hōshin (disengaging mind). In terms of martial arts, if the mind gets stuck with one opponent, another may catch you unawares. While a brief moment of zanshin is indispensable, it is equally necessary to disengage the mind in time.

A Goal, A Path

Always practice with an objective in mind. The objective will vary from person to person, but never practice without one. Do not try to win or look good. Aim higher. Imagine rails in front of you. To reach the next station you need to move along the rails. You can only find the way if you have a goal. Otherwise, you will stumble all over the place without getting anywhere. O-Sensei walked wherever he wanted, and rather than in front of him, a clear path formed behind him. O-Sensei was able to do this, achieving what I would call the greatest possible freedom. But for most of us I believe it is important to practice with a goal in mind. Only if you find your own objective and work on it, only if you move at your own pace, and in your own direction - not to win or show off but simply to harmonize with yourself, others, and nature - a miracle will happen, and you will draw a path behind you like a boat in the water, a path so clear others will find it and follow you.

What is 合気 Aiki?

To understand 合気 aiki, examine both aspects of your practice: practicing for yourself and practicing for your partner. When you practice for yourself, focus on controlling the attack and getting yourself into a safe place without considering the consequences for your partner. This is a typical martial rationale. When you practice for your partner, focus on being caring, protective, respectful and loving towards him. Think of your partner as your baby. When he attacks, put him to sleep. Do not slam his head on the ground or allow anybody to harm him. You need to make sure he is safe and comfortable. You need to maintain a stable posture and watch your surroundings so nobody can attack the baby that relies on you for safety. Together, these two aspects form aiki, the principle of harmony. Both are equally important. Isolating the two types of practice now and then sharpens our mind and body to what each of them entails. We need to find the right balance between them to live with integrity, respect and love, while we also let our partner live with integrity, respect and love. This is aiki, our chosen path.

Look at the Sky

Every once in a while, take a look at the sky.
Look at it for only a second, then close your
eyes and remember what you saw. Which
direction were the clouds moving? How
many birds did you see? When I look at the
sky at night, I notice the moon. The stars.
The clouds. But what about the rest of the
sky? How much of the vast, dark sky do we
actually see? I, too, have the tendency to
look at the sky and think: 'What a beautiful
moon!' But the moon is only beautiful
because the sky is dark. We can only
breathe out because we breathe in. We
point at the other side of the earth, but
at the same time, we point at the sky
above it. This is an important teaching
in aikido. There are 表技 omote-waza
(forward techniques) and 裏技 ura-waza
(backward techniques). Each one of us is
the center of the universe. The world is
as big as we make it.

自然体 Shizentai for Freedom and Peace

'Shizentai' means 'natural body' or 'natural posture' but achieving it takes a lot of effort. This is the effort Zen practitioners call 只管打坐 shikantaza.

Miyamoto Musashi said: '有構無構' yūkō mukō (kamae is no kamae). Do not expect a certain attack. Keep your posture straight, neither aggressive nor defensive, neither arrogant nor timid. This promotes a peaceful state of mind. Japanese yakuza often walk hunched over. They get into a lot of fights. If you walk straight, your arms swinging back and forth naturally, it is unlikely that you will be drawn into a fight.

Musashi also said: '見の目弱く、観の目強く' ken no me yowaku, kan no me tsuyoku (weak eyes, strong antennae). If you focus on your partner too much you will not be ready for attacks from other people. If you watch your partner's right hand too closely, you will not be ready for attacks from his left hand. Do not focus on one thing in particular. Look at everything at once. Use your antennae.

Striving for shizentai leads towards freedom and peace of mind.

Shizentai Checklist

自然体 shizentai literally means 'natural body', or 'natural posture'. But we have to work hard to find it and maintain it at all times. This is one of the most important issues in aikido. We need to be strict with ourselves.

Shizentai consists of the following aspects:

- Eyes: look at everything equally, not just at one thing
- Back: shoulder blades together and down
- Shoulders: always relaxed - Breathing: always calm, in coordination with your movements
- Ki: emanating freely from your body, flowing in whatever direction you decide
- Knees: always relaxed, ready to move in any direction
- Mind: always calm and open for whatever may happen (水の心 mizu no kokoro - mind of water)

If you use this checklist you can gradually approach shizentai. Shizentai is the most simple, yet the most difficult thing to achieve. While we should have faith that it exists in us, we need to keep practicing and actively guide our body and mind towards it. Shizentai is perfect freedom.

Shizentai for the Back

Many people let their shoulders slump. If you walk hunched over, your hands stay in front of your body. This is the yakuza way of walking. Yakuza get into a lot of fights. If you put your shoulder blades close to your spine and slide them down, your back becomes straight, and when you walk, your hands naturally swing back and forth by your sides. Your ki can emanate freely. Walking straight and upright helps avoid fights. Another aspect of this is what Miyamoto Musashi described as 有構無構 yūkō mukō (kamae is no kamae). A neutral starting position and an open mind allow full freedom of reaction should you be unexpectedly attacked. Keep your back straight, even in the process of sitting down or standing up. If you sit down with your back straight and cross your legs, you find yourself in zazen position. This is the posture of the Buddha. The Buddha uses many 印 in (hand gestures), but he always sits with his back straight. This is shizentai for the back. Shoulder blades together and down. Back straight.

Shizentai for the Shoulders

Sometimes when you concentrate hard on keeping your back straight, your shoulders tense up. It is important to always relax your shoulders. Some attacks make this difficult. If you feel uncomfortable with the way your partner twists your arm and disturbs your balance, step into a position that makes it easier to relax your shoulders. Do not think about throwing your partner. Remember, he is very dear to you. Simply find the right position and relax your shoulders. This is enough to break your partner's balance. If you try to move only your hand, you will end up using strength, and your partner will fight back. This is not aikido. Move from your center and relax your shoulders. Your hand is only a prop that cannot work on its own. If your shoulders are tense, you are not in control and cannot do things at your own pace. When your shoulders are tense, your range of movement is limited. Always relax your shoulders. This is shizentai for the shoulders.

Shizentai for the Eyes

When getting attacked, we have a tendency to look only at our attacker, his hand, or his weapon. This limited view makes us feel intimidated, shrink back, and become tense in body and mind. If our partner is in front of us, we automatically look at him and adjust our movement to his. But in aikido, we should adjust ki to ki. Adjust to his first thought of attack, which occurs before his first movement. Do not be tempted to look at his face, fist, or weapon. Look at everything equally. Include your partner in your field of vision as one of many components. Miyamoto Musashi said: 見の目弱く、観の目強く Ken no me yowaku, kan no me tsuyoku. The eye of ken is weak. The eye of kan is strong. 見 ken refers to our actual sense of vision. 観 kan refers to the antenna-like power of ki, a kind of instinct or 6th sense we can sharpen through practice. Expand your field of vision. Make your world bigger. This is shizentai for the eyes: a wide field of vision. Looking at everything equally.

Shizentai for the Knees

Sometimes your knees tense up, and you end up locking them. From this position it is impossible to move quickly. Always make sure your knees are relaxed, ready to move in any direction. To move your body you need your feet. To move your feet you need your legs, and to move your legs you need your knees. Think of the steering wheel in a car. It needs to be ready to move whenever you decide to steer the car in a new direction. In the same way, your knees should be ready to operate smoothly and immediately whenever you want to move your body. Be aware of this and keep your knees in a relaxed state that allows for swift, free maneuvering. This is shizentai for the knees. Always keep your knees relaxed and ready to move.

Shizentai for 気 ki

Your power in aikido comes from projecting 気 ki, concentrated in the lower abdomen. If you move towards your partner hunched over, with tense muscles, or breathing haphazardly you cannot control the way you project ki. This easily gives rise to resistance from your partner and brings out your tendency to use strength trying to compensate for the missing power of ki. This type of encounter is a digression from what we try to achieve in aikido. The more you move from your center, and the better you learn to project ki, the less strength you will need to achieve effective techniques. In addition, always send out your best possible 外気 gaiki (external ki - the ki you send out). Sending out good gaiki to your partner means feeling grateful towards him, giving him a warm welcome, and making him feel safe and appreciated. Two partners sending out good gaiki to each other will achieve the best possible technique at their skill level and through this harmonious exchange, feel good 内気 naiki - internal ki - as a result. This is shizentai for ki. Keep your ki calm and centered. Nurture good ki, and learn to control and project it.

Breathing Shizentai

Breathing properly is a vital aspect of shizentai. Your breathing should always be calm, your exhale longer than your inhale. Breathing should be an organic part of your movements. What is the difference between an artificial and a real flower? Both look beautiful. But an artificial flower has no scent. A flower's scent shows that it is alive. It is similar with aikido techniques. A technique may look correct, but if it lacks the power of breathing, it is not alive. When you do a technique, start with the objective of breathing in not only your partner, but the entire universe. Sometimes you get attacked before you can adjust your breathing. You get stuck. Your partner holds you tight and twists you into an uncomfortable position. One way of getting out of this is to simply stay where you are, use your breath to relax your shoulders, return to shizentai, and make your partner sink with your breath. This is a form of ki - training used in aikido. Control your breathing and use it harmoniously with your movements. This is shizentai for your breath.

Breathing It In

One mistake I often notice is that people focus too much on their partner. With this, they create a very small, limited world. They think about nothing but their partner and his hand. Their only concerns are: 'How can I move his hand?' and 'How can I throw him?' Think outside the box. Create a circle of ki. Put your partner inside your circle, your sphere of influence. Absorb the attack. Only then are you free to do with it what you want. If you reject the attack, you will never be able to control it. When you breathe your partner into your sphere, do not absorb your partner only. With gratitude and devotion, breathe in your partner, the earth, the stars, and the universe.

Getting up and Sitting Down

In both Zen and aikido, 自然体 shizentai (natural posture) is a central theme. Pay attention to shizentai even when engaging in simple movements you perform every day. Getting up and sitting down, for example. When getting up and sitting down, many people bend over and carelessly use their limbs or other people and objects around them to support their crumpled postures. During this simple action, they lose all grace and dignity. Even in the process of standing up or sitting down, maintain good posture, shoulder blades together and down. When you sit down, simply descend. When you get up, simply rise. Rise from the abdomen, not from the legs. It may seem easier to support yourself as you straighten your crooked posture and get up sloppily, but try to keep your upper body straight when getting up or sitting down. It may seem difficult at first, but if you keep practicing you will find that your movements have become more comfortable and more stable. The idea is to maintain shizentai at all times, whether you get up or sit down, whether you stand still or move.

Big World,
Small World,
Your
World

For a good katame (pin), all you have to
do is be in the right place and maintain
shizentai: straight, good posture. Then,
form a circle with your arms and turn up
your palms, feeling the whole earth inside
your center. If you do this, it is impossible
for your partner to get up, but he does not
feel angry or irritated about being in this
position. He does not think 'I have been
defeated!', so he will not fight back. This is
because you are maintaining shizentai.
Your world is big. If you try with all your
might to push down your partner's arm,
you narrow down your world and your
sphere of influence. As soon as you fight,
your partner can feel it. He becomes
irritated, fights back, and can easily get
up because now you are not maintaining
shizentai. You are focusing on nothing
but one tiny detail. Your world is small.
Expand your world. Expand your sphere
of influence. If you are the universe,
nothing can go against you.

Heavenly Dango

Every one of you is the center of the universe. O-Sensei said 'I am a microcosm of the universe.' O-Sensei was able to live this truth. He had truly understood it. If you are the universe, nothing can stand in your way. Everything in your experience becomes the universe. You are in control. This is why many people believe O-Sensei was a god. O-Sensei liked dango, sticky, sweet rice balls, which are a popular treat in Japan. The most common variety are sakura-dango (cherry blossom rice balls): three dango, pink, white, and green on a wooden skewer. We eat them at cherry blossom picnics in spring. But O-Sensei's dango were exceptionally big. The dango he ate were the sun, the moon, and the earth. He sprinkled some stardust on them and enjoyed his treat. Maybe if you try this snack, you will feel a little bigger. This is how big I want you to feel. Each one of you is a microcosm of the universe. Once you manage to perceive yourself as the universe and create harmony, there will be no more fighting.

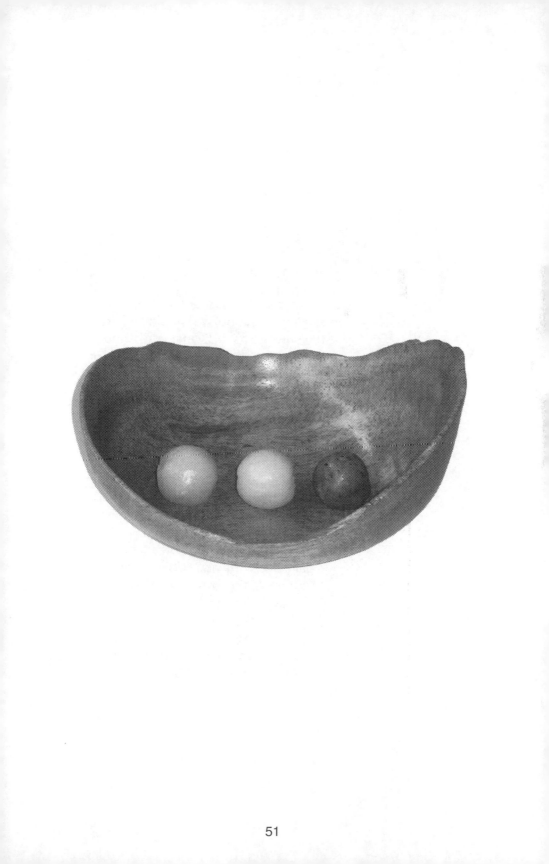

Molt and Breathe

Each of us is a microcosm of the universe. To eliminate fighting, we should feel like the universe itself. Even if you cannot immediately accomplish this, approach your goal step by step. Start with small things. Do not look only at your partner or focus on pushing him down. Widen your focus. Try to keep your axis stable, and things will start revolving around you more smoothly. Leave your limited world behind step by step. Every time you manage to take one step further towards a big world, you resemble a snake that sheds its skin in order to grow. Like the snake, molt again and again. Keep growing. When you do a technique, do not simply breathe in the air around you. Like a freshly molted snake that now has space to breathe again, stretch your lungs, breathe in the air, your partner, the stars, and the earth. Breathe in the whole universe.

Using 100%

Miyamoto Musashi fought with two swords. But he did not always use both. He would use each sword as appropriate. If he had a lot of space, he would use the long sword, if he was fighting in a confined space, he would use the short sword. Only if the situation called for it, he would use both. When you actively push your partner down, you overuse your hand, and it becomes a throwing hand. Instead of 100% you are using 120%. Musashi said: 'Whatever means you have, use them to the fullest.' This does not mean using 120%. It means using exactly 100%. It means using only what is necessary, no more, no less. Use body and mind efficiently. Any other weapons are merely extensions of body and mind. Musashi also said: 'When I have a sword, I don't rely on it, so not having a sword doesn't faze me.' Using a weapon to the fullest means retaining the courage to throw it away at any moment if the situation demands it.

Enter Through Form

Musashi's phrase: 'Kamae is no kamae' describes shizentai, a natural, straight posture that allows ki to emanate from your body easily and gives you the greatest possible freedom. Shizentai is what we strive for in both Zen and aikido. If you tidy up your posture, this will tidy up your mind, and vice versa. However, it is difficult to tidy up your mind, so in both Zen and aikido we try to work on our posture first. We enter through form. Tidy up your mind through correct form. Take off your shoes and arrange them neatly, composing your mind before you step onto the mat. Bow correctly, and your mind will follow with correct attitude. This is why children learn about posture and etiquette. We work on achieving correct form every time we practice. This is the true meaning of practice. Whether you practice aikido, Zen, flower arrangement, or tea ceremony - all these systems are 道 dō, paths, which provide forms we can practice to tidy up our mind. Mind and form are like two wheels on an axle. They work as one. Entering through form is our best bet to make progress.

Correct Form, Correct Attitude

In Zen, we say that correct attitude follows correct form. When you come into the dojo, you bow at the entrance. You walk up to the mat, take off your shoes and place them neatly in the shoe shelf or in front of the mat. All these things are part of the material world. They are formalities. But through performing these actions correctly, you correct your attitude even before you step onto the mat. At the same time, correct attitude also leads to correct form. If you feel truly grateful to your partner for practicing with you, you will be able to absorb him into your sphere, achieve harmony with him, and perform beautiful techniques with good posture. Pay attention to both attitude and form. In this way, one will correct the other. Inside, feel acceptance and gratefulness. Judging from experience, this is the more difficult part. So make sure you work with correct posture and observe etiquette. This will help you establish and maintain correct attitude.

Respectful Alignment

When I sit down in front of founder O-Sensei Ueshiba at the beginning of class, I align my center with his, so my center line becomes a continuation of his center line. When you sit down in front of the founder, align your center with his, face him and feel as close to him as if you could talk to him or practice with him any minute. When you sit down in front of your teacher, do the same. Align your center with his. This is a form of Japanese etiquette, a symbol of your promise to do what it takes to internalize your teacher's skill and knowledge, to give new life to them through your own efforts, and to allow your teacher's essence to continue through your own life and work.

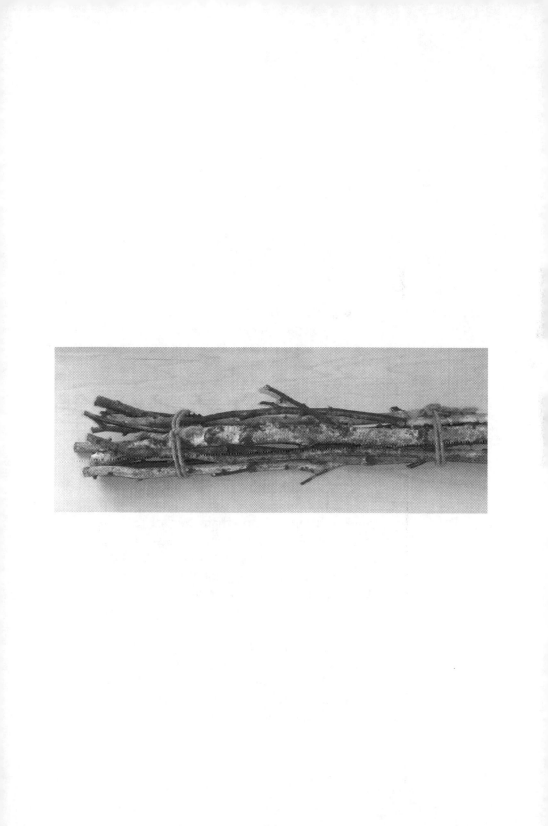

The Meaning of Prayer

合掌 gasshō is the prayer pose we use in Zen. The two characters mean 'unite' and 'palms'. In gasshō we unite our palms in front of our chest, fingers pointing up. When praying, it is important to relax and maintain shizentai. Do not squeeze your hands together or let your shoulders get tense. Follow correct form and relax. In gasshō your hands are said to become a lotus flower, which carries in its midst the Buddha that lives inside you. There are two components to prayer, symbolized by the two hands. This concept is called 願誓 gansei, written with the characters for 'request' and 'pledge'. With one hand, you ask for help. You seek assistance in fulfilling your wish from entities whose power is greater than your own. With the other hand, you make a pledge. You promise that you will do your best to move actively towards your goal - that you will eat healthy, study harder, never forget her birthday again, or do whatever else it may take to reach your goal. When praying, our hands unite the humble search for help with the genuine promise to make an effort.

Treasure Each Encounter

Every day we should make a sincere effort to connect with our fellow human beings and treasure each encounter. Speaking in terms of aikido, from inviting our partner in, to the first actual touch, to the last moment of zanshin, treasure each encounter. There should be a feeling of importance and gravity to accepting an attack. You should neither take it lightly nor run away from it or let it shrink you. Accept it gratefully, without resistance. Be strict with yourself and grace your partner with the touch of kindness. Only then can you process the attack correctly, at your own pace, without losing your balance. Only then a smooth, harmonious connection will be born between you and your partner. Only then can you truly treasure the encounter and emerge victorious in the true sense of the word: you have fully accepted the attack and dealt with it to the best of your abilities while strictly observing yourself in the process and prioritizing victory against your own weaknesses over striking down your partner. After the encounter, thank your partner and reflect upon what you could do better next time to achieve perfect harmony.

不動心
Fudōshin
and 無心
Mushin

不動心 'fudōshin' is written with the characters:
'no', 'move', and 'mind'. It can be translated as
'immovable mind' or 'Zen mind'. 'Immovable',
however, does not mean 'rigid'. Its meaning is
closer to 'calm' - a free mind that cannot be
shaken. In Zen, the mind is often compared
with water. If the surface of a lake is rippled,
the reflection of the moon gets distorted and
does not resemble the real moon. Equally, if
your mind is full of distractions, the reality it
perceives becomes distorted. If the surface of
the lake is calm, the reflection of the moon
becomes the real moon's spitting image.
Equally, if your mind is calm, you can
perceive your environment's true nature.
無心 mushin is a related concept written
with the characters 'no' and 'mind' but it
does not mean 'mindless'. Like fudōshin,
it expresses an ultimately calm state of
mind. As soon as the emptiness of the
mind is perfect, the world flows in and
fills it. Only then, no longer distracted
by hope, fear, and other expectations,
can we react to things immediately
and take each moment as it comes.

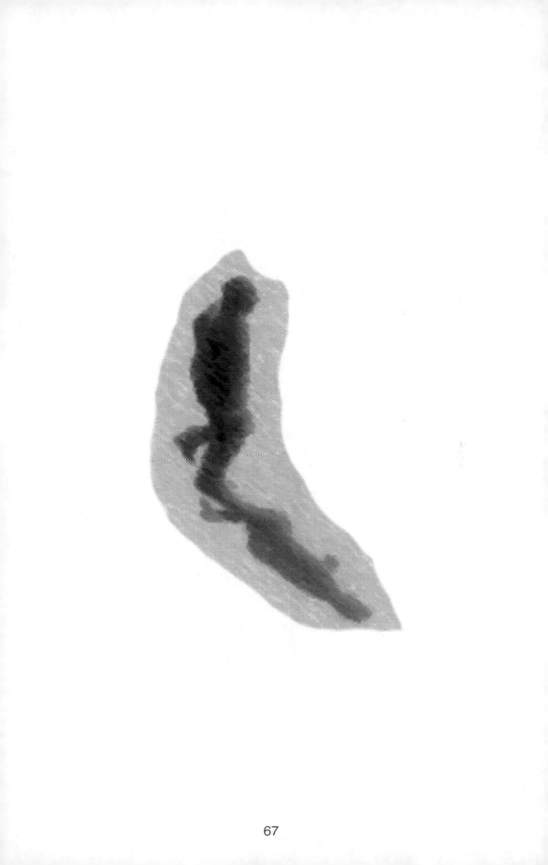

God Inside, Peace Inside

The theory we embrace in Zen is that God is not a separate being. The divine exists inside us. If we empty ourselves of egocentric thoughts, this Buddha-nature will fill us, and we will become one with nature and the universe. When you practice zazen correctly, nothing can shake you. Whatever happens, you can accept it and let it be. In aikido this means: whatever attack you get, accept it, and it cannot harm you. You can control the consequences of its impact with your attitude. If you achieve 不動心 fudōshin (immovable mind), nothing can disturb your peace of mind.

不動心 Fudōshin, 平常心 Heijōshin, and 一味禅 Ichimizen

Remaining calm whatever happens is the kind of freedom we try to achieve in aikido. Whether your opponent is holding a sword, a spear, or a machine gun, whether he is weak or strong, beautiful or ugly, young or old, whether you are starved or stuffed, whether the sun is scorching or the rain pouring - do not let anything or anybody cut your ki. In other words, do not let anything faze you. Remain calm at all times. This calm state of mind is called 不動心 fudōshin (immovable mind) or 平常心 heijōshin (normal mind), meaning that nothing can disturb your peace of mind, openness of perception, and freedom to act and react. If we apply this universally to the many different aspects and situations of our lives, this is called 一味禅 ichimizen, written with the characters for 'one', 'flavor', and 'Zen'. This is what we should try to do. Aikido is not limited to what we do in the dojo. Our practice of aikido should affect the way we behave outside the dojo in our daily lives.

不動心 Fudōshin vs The 3-Part-Attack

不動心 Fudōshin (the immovable mind) is more reliable than your eyes. Teach your eyes to serve fudōshin. There are 3 parts to any attack. To use the sword as an example, first, the thought occurs to cut - stage 1. Next, the sword is lifted - stage 2. Finally, the sword comes down - stage 3. It is the same with a gun. 1 - The thought occurs to shoot. 2 - The trigger is pulled. 3 - The bullet is fired. Becoming aware of an attack at stage 3 is too late. Detecting it during stage 2 is still dangerous. Best is to catch it at stage 1. If your mind is calm you can feel the waves made by your partner's intention to attack. If you look at your partner your focus will be broken. You will be taken in by his eyes, his weapon, or his fighting stance. Do not look at your partner. Make your field of vision as wide as possible. Your partner is only one component in your field of vision. In this way, your eyes can serve fudōshin, and fudōshin can serve you.

Receive

When you are the one being attacked,
invite your partner in. Do not wait for him
to attack. Encounter him with a sincere
feeling of gratefulness and a genuine
desire to create harmony between you.
You are very important. Hold yourself
dear. Your partner is equally important.
Hold your partner dear. Every technique
is important - we should try to do every
technique as perfectly as we can, extracting
from our personalities our best possible
selves. So in this sense, hold each technique
dear, too. If you pay attention to all three
components - self, partner and technique -
this will result in beautiful aikido. To
receive something is not simply to
wait for it, but to pick it up.

Reflect

Everybody has their own goals when practicing aikido. But there are some basic components we should all strive for. When doing a technique, try to achieve harmony with your partner and send him your best possible ki. While paying attention to this, your aikido will improve with time as you repeatedly practice the techniques. Getting better at aikido is the result rather than the objective of your practice. After completing a technique, reflect on the following questions: Is your partner where you want him to be? Are you where you want to be? Is your posture good? Are you in control? Is your partner safe? Are you safe? Did you both enjoy the technique? Reflect and keep practicing. The aim of your reflections is that, as you keep practicing, you will be able to answer more and more of these questions with 'Yes'.

Aim

If you could actually be the universe
and execute limitless techniques, you
would no longer be yourself, so you
cannot really achieve this while being
human. But what we can all do is aim
to become the universe and aim for
our techniques to become limitless.
This quest must never stop. It is the
best we can do to achieve harmony.

Keep Your Hair

When somebody pulls your hair your natural impulse is trying to separate the attacker from you by pulling his hand off your head. But this hurts. Instead, accept the attack. Put your hands on his with a feeling of gratefulness, as if accepting a present. Gently press against your head, sandwiching the attacker's hand between your head and hands. Then, simply bow. As you bow, the attacker will fly over your head. The example of hair-pulling is a principle we should always keep in mind. Somebody attacks. Your first impulse is to push or pull him away from you. But remember, this hurts. Accept the attack. Keep his hand, keep your hair. As soon as you bow 'Thank you!' your problem will be solved. Acceptance is the first step towards an effective solution. If you do not accept unwelcome influences you let them roam free, allowing them to work their way into your life at their own pace. Accept them. Show them respect and gratefulness, and they will fly right over your head.

Three Levels of Victory

Sun Tzu said: There are three levels of victory. The lowest level is to simply fight your opponent and win. The next level is to prepare yourself well, make sure you have the advantage and then fight your opponent and win. But the highest level of victory is to win without fighting. This is what we try to achieve in aikido.

True Aikido Victory

We are human beings with human weaknesses. It often seems easier to get up, sit down, or walk in a sloppy manner than to make an effort and maintain correct posture. Often, we throw our partner to the ground using all the muscle strength we have. We bend backwards or hold our breath when countering an attack. These are only some of our weaknesses. But remember that in aikido, we do not try to win against our partner. This kind of victory is meaningless. In aikido, we try to win against our own weaknesses. We try to win against ourselves. Only this kind of victory is truly meaningful.

Posture, Field of Vision, Breathing

Posture, field of vision, and breathing are the three vital ingredients for good aikido. First, posture. Put your shoulder blades together and down. Next, field of vision. Musashi said: 'Do not look your opponent in the eyes. Make your field of vision wide, and include your opponent in the multitude of things you see.' Musashi also thought it would be beneficial to reduce blinking. To do this, he said, pull the insides of your eyebrows together and narrow your eyes. In my opinion it is best to do things as naturally as possible, but sometimes little tricks like this can help you achieve certain goals, like widening your field of vision. Third, breathing. If you breathe fast and hard, your shoulders are likely to become tense, and you cannot perform techniques in a relaxed, efficient manner. Make sure your breathing matches your movement. Try to breathe calmly and evenly. This makes it easier to detect your partner's intentions. As a general rule of thumb, breathe in when you welcome your partner's attack. Breathe out when you redirect him. This will help your techniques flow.

道
Michi /
Dō

In Japan, we have many paths, all designed to help human beings better themselves continuously and progress ceaselessly towards achieving their highest potential. Aikido is one of these paths. The word 'path' is written with the character 道. On its own it is usually pronounced 'michi', in combination with other characters 'dō'. A path is not a path if only certain people can walk it. A path is walkable for anybody. But what does it mean to walk a path? There are two important aspects to it. One is 稽古 keiko, which refers to practicing the old ways and imitating the refined forms our predecessors have handed down to us. The second aspect is to create our own path. We are all individuals and need to custom tailor our paths to our needs. Once you begin to walk your own path with faith and confidence, a new path will appear behind you like the lines drawn by a boat in the water. When your path becomes clear, others will follow you. If you make mistakes building your path, assess them honestly and fix the damage. Do not neglect either one of these aspects. Build and walk with respect.

What is 気 Ki?

When you ask me what 気 ki is, my answer is: ki is prayer. When you pray for people's health to get better, you are sending them ki. When you bow and greet your partner before and after practice, you emit ki. When you pray, you send ki to the power you pray to, and to the goal of your prayer. When you move with centered, smoothly flowing ki, you can move the things around you as if they were part of you. Through focusing and directing your ki you are in touch with the universe. Ki is prayer.

外気 Gaiki, 内気 Naiki, and 雰囲気 Funiki

In Japanese the word 雰囲気 funiki (atmosphere) contains the character 気 ki - the essential energy we use to express ourselves and communicate in aikido. If we send out bad ki, our surroundings will receive this signal and darken. If we send out bright, positive ki on the other hand, we can create a good atmosphere. 外気 gaiki (external ki) is the ki we send out. It is our responsibility to send out the best, happiest, most grateful ki we can at all times. If both partners do this in aikido, their gaiki will form a harmonious spiral, and the resulting harmony will resonate positively within them, creating good 内気 naiki (internal ki), as well as a good 雰囲気 funiki (atmosphere). Send out your best energy to the people around you. This will help you and everybody else feel better.

The Power of Water

When water hits sand, it seeps into it. When it meets a cup, it fills the cup. It flows from the mountains and fills the oceans. It moulds rocks. It rinses out dirt. It creates and destroys life. It incorporates objects into its flow and keeps moving at its own pace. Water is free. We often use the power of water to describe what we aspire to in the martial arts. 水の心 mizu no kokoro (mind of water) is a crystal clear mind like a lake's still surface. When the water is calm, the moon is reflected in it perfectly. When waves appear, the image is distorted. Equally, when your mind is calm, it perfectly reflects reality, giving you a strong center. When shaken up, it distorts reality, thwarting appropriate reactions. 気の流れ ki no nagare (ki flow) is ki flowing like water. It can rinse out your weaknesses. It can flush away the impact of your partner's attacks. Use whatever space opens up to you, without trying to resist. The forces you meet guide you towards no resistance. Emulate water to create harmony. Keep mind and body calm and flow.

Harmony – Not Sameness but Kindness

The Japanese word 和不同 wafudō, written with the characters 'harmony', 'not', and 'same' expresses that harmony does not equal sameness. On the contrary, for the concept of harmony to exist, it takes multiple factors, multiple forces, multiple notes. When we try to create harmony with our partner, we do not try to become the same person. We respect each other, including all our differences, and try to complement each other in the most harmonious way, bringing out each other's best. For harmony, we need kindness (優しさ yasashisa) and love (愛 ai). Your intentions towards your partner should be kind and loving. In the same vein, you should be considerate towards your partner. The concept of mutual consideration is called 思いやり omoiyari. As human beings, we need to be considerate and take good care of each other in order to create harmony.

Harmony of Flavors

In Japan, we have a type of dish called '和え物' (aemono), written with the characters for 'harmony' and 'thing'. Aemono usually combines two ingredients. Often, one of the ingredients alone would not taste good. It may be too bitter, too oily, or too dry. But combined with the other, its best flavors are brought to the fore, while its negative components exert a positive influence upon the first ingredient and bring out its most delicious flavors. If you eat only toasted bread, it is too dry. If you eat only butter, it is too oily. But when you spread butter on warm toast, the bread sucks up the oiliness of the butter, the butter moistens the dryness of the bread, and the result is perfect harmony. Try to harmonize with your partner in the same way. Put everything you have into your practice. Even your weaknesses have the potential to turn into something beautiful when combined with the characteristics of your partner. With the right effort, even your flaws can contribute to the creation of harmony.

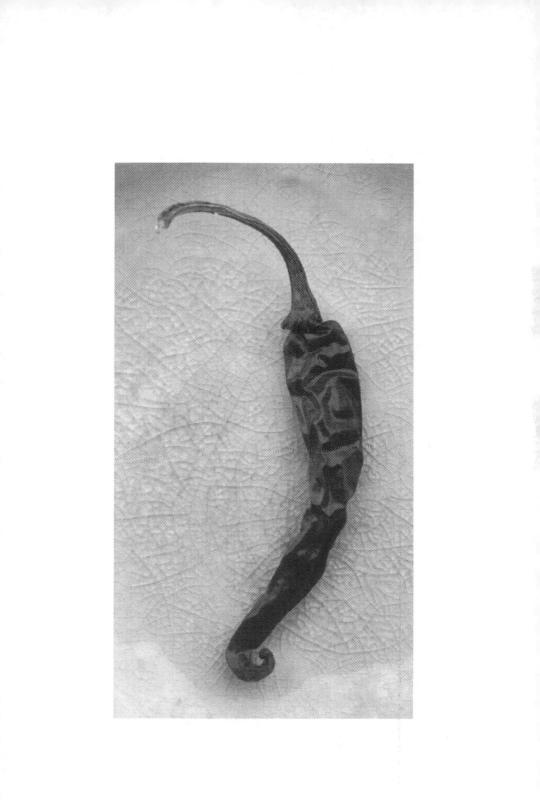

Be Yourself and Respect Others

In aikido, we want to create 和合 wagō, harmony. The character 和 wa can mean 'harmony', but it can also mean 'plus'. When you work with your partner, add your characteristics to his. This does not mean that you become one and the same person. You both remain intact and distinct. But by putting your characteristics together, you can create true harmony.

There is an old Chinese saying that goes:

大人は和して同ぜず   taijin ha washite dōzezu
小人は同じて和せず   shōjin ha dōjite wasezu

Big souls stand apart in harmony
Respecting each other's place.
Small souls know no harmony
However much they chatter and hug.

My uke and I have completely different personalities but I respect him and accept whatever he gives me. I welcome him into my sphere. This is what you should aim for when you practice. If you get it right, it will feel good for both partners and any onlookers. After practice you should think: 'This was fun, I want to go again!' Not: 'This was hard, I don't know if I'll go next time.'

Strict Practice Leads to Gentleness

Sometimes your techniques come out hard and strong. A lot of the time, such techniques do not work very well. As you make progress, your techniques will usually become softer and more gentle. They will also become more effective. You will acquire a higher level of efficiency - less effort, more effect. But this cannot be achieved in one day. You have to be strict with yourself. Practice hard and persistently over a long period of time. Practice shizentai. Practice accepting the attack. Practice maintaining a stable axis. Display a caring attitude towards your partner without losing focus or balance. Do not throw your partner in order to throw him. Use him to win against your own flaws. When you master all this, you may choose to execute faster techniques that appear strong and vigorous. But no matter how fast, all good techniques contain the basic building blocks listed above. All good techniques have gentleness at their root. Gentleness takes a lot of practice. Be strict with yourself and gentle with your partner.

天地人 Ten Chi Jin – Heaven, Earth, Man

天地投げ tenchi-nage means heaven-earth throw. One hand snakes up, stretching endlessly into the sky like a dragon, while the other snakes down burrowing endlessly into the earth. This technique is a symbol for the fact that heaven, earth, and man are connected, as in the word 天地人 ten chi jin (heaven, earth, man). As human beings, we have the responsibility to be the best possible link between heaven and earth. When we achieve this, heaven, earth, and man dissolve. O-Sensei taught us to finish irimi-nage by pointing our fingers down. The same happens with the bottom hand in tenchi-nage. But if you think about it, your hand is pointing at the other side of the earth. Above the earth is the sky again, so you are also pointing at the sky. The pointing hand symbolizes infinity and our connection with it. In aikido, we try to connect with nature, with heaven, earth, and our partner. Every time you practice, be aware of this. The fingers you use to complete the technique are not simply pointing down. They are stretching towards infinity.

A Great Machine

Our body is a perfectly functioning
machine. Its parts work together
harmoniously like the gear wheels
in a clockwork. Whatever you do, it
is this great machine that makes it
possible. Even when malfunctions
occur, we cannot even grasp just how
well all our parts are designed, how
masterfully they are put together,
and how smoothly they work as a
team. Be grateful for this natural
perfection and harmony. Each
one of you is a microcosm of
the universe.

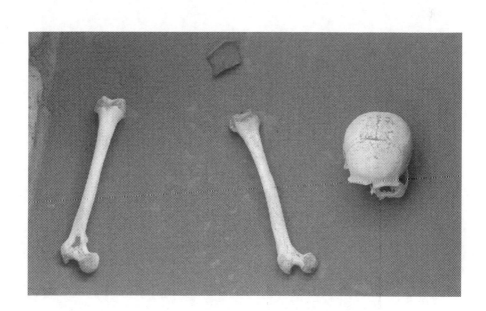

Whatever There Is

Do you ever look at the sky and invite
it into your heart? Do you ever breathe
in the scent of a flower and appreciate
its life? Do you think this sounds easy?
Then do it. Once a day. Breathe. Look
at the sky. Look at planes, birds, clouds,
and appreciate whatever there is. It
will help you find peace.

Three Steps to the Universe

First, you have to practice technique - the mechanics of interacting with your partner. But perfecting your technique is not enough. Next, you have to become sensitive to your partner's wishes, and honor them. Hold your partner dear. Respect him. With each interaction get to know him better, get to know him anew. Every moment, let him be what he is. Mastering this will make you more advanced, but it is still not enough. Finally, you need to learn how to be in control at all times. You should be in control even before your partner attacks. Invite him to give you a certain attack and he will. Once you reach this level you are the universe, and the concept of fighting ceases to exist.

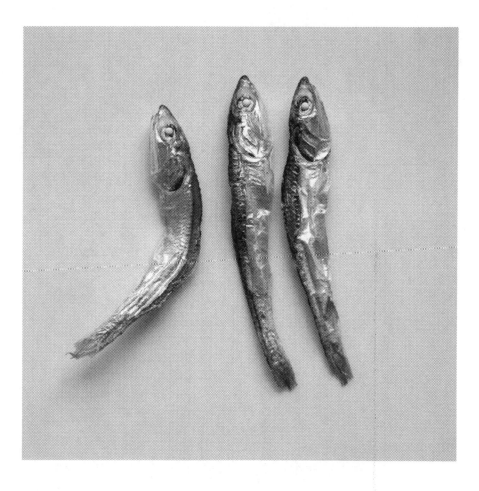

Castle
with
Moat

Think of yourself as a beautiful castle with a moat around it. In this way you can stand proud and will not be fazed by any attack. Dispersing your worries, detaching yourself from them, and winning against their negative influence in this way is called 吾勝 agatsu. Do not try to start a war from your castle. Simply take good care of it and do not let conflict arise within its walls. The only victory you should strive for is victory against your own weaknesses - victory against yourself. This type of victory is called 正勝 masakatsu (true victory). Working towards victory in the sense of 正勝吾勝 masakatsu agatsu ensures that your castle will stand strong, beautiful, and undefeated. If you genuinely work on winning against your weaknesses in daily life, your castle will succeed in spreading harmony across the land and across its borders.

Antennae

Insects have feelers - antennae that allow them to perceive what is going on around them. If their antennae fail to work, this is a matter of life and death for them. TVs have antennae. School children have antennae for listening to their teachers. I taught at a junior high school for 30 years. After I taught my students about antennae, their grades improved. This is not surprising. As human beings, we do not have one antenna like a TV or two like an insect. But we have the potential to acquire an all-round antenna system picking up signals from all directions. To achieve this, however, we need to work on it. Focus. Think big. Even when you get attacked, do not let it shrink your mind and body. Do not let a single thought dominate your world while losing focus of the overall picture. Double-check your attitude and win against your own tendency to become small-minded. In this way we need to constantly work on our antenna system. It needs to be polished in order to work. Keep your antennae sharp and your picture clear.

A
Good
Place

In aikido as in life, direct your efforts towards being in a good place. From the beginning, think about the place you are going to take in each encounter. Put yourself in a place where you can easily absorb your partner's attack. Assume the best possible position at all times. One important aspect of this is 間合 maai (distance). Even before the encounter starts, pay attention to angle and distance. If you are in the wrong place, your partner can attack however he likes and easily dominate you. Make sure you position yourself at a distance and angle that allow you to work at your own pace, and prevent your partner from attacking in a way that complicates your defense. It is simple. Be in the right place at the right time.

Relishing the Energy of a Place

On the one hand, your practice should be the same wherever you are. In this sense, seminar practice is nothing unusual. On the other hand, every place has its own individual qualities, so especially when you practice in a new environment, try to appreciate it. Connect your feet well with the ground you stand on, and breathe in large lungfuls of the air around you. Open the crown of your head to the sky, and try to send out the ki that is now combining your individual qualities with the special qualities of this location, through every pore of your body. This allows you to bring out and relish the qualities of the place hosting you at each given moment, and even though you practice just as diligently as usual, the result may differ from place to place.

Inviting the Attack

Osawa Sensei's movements were extremely soft and gentle, but very effective. He stressed that it was important not to wait for your partner's attack, but to invite it and welcome it with all your heart. Invite your partner in and let him do what he wants, but your way. Take irimi-nage, for example. First, your partner attacks from above. His arm wants to go down, so let it go down. Next, he wants to get up, so let him get up. Then, he is bent backwards. The easiest way out is down. Let him go down. This way, the technique is smooth and harmonious, and your partner ends up on the ground. In aikido we listen to each other and create harmony. We respect each other but never forget that we are individuals with distinct personalities practicing a martial art. While performing a technique, two separate individuals complement each other to create a unit of harmony. Invite your partner. Welcome him in. Breathe him in and accept him, breathe him out and send him on his way.

啐啄 Sottaku – Nurturing

'Knock, knock!' goes the mother's beak on the outside of the egg. But not to break it. The egg needs to be broken from the inside. The chick has to do it with its own soft beak - a task assigned by nature. But the parent bird needs to plant the idea in the chick's head. Without the hen's knocking, the chick would never think of breaking the shell. The hen knocks, the chick responds. Parent nurtures child. Effort brings forth effort, until finally, the chick hammers its way through the shell and smashes into the world, where parent and child meet for the first time. This is 啐啄 sottaku 同時 dōji. Both characters in 'sottaku' contain the character 'mouth' on the left. The right side of the first character means 'graduate'. 'Dōji' means 'at the same time'. Parent and child put forth their parental and filial spirit simultaneously, thus revealing each other's presence. This mutual stimulation, respect, attention, and response is what we aim to achieve in aikido.

Softness Needs a Center

If you try to do techniques softly without using your center, your softness will be weak. But softness with a center is strong. Make sure you always remember this important difference. Doing soft techniques is good. But to make them succeed your center needs to be stable.

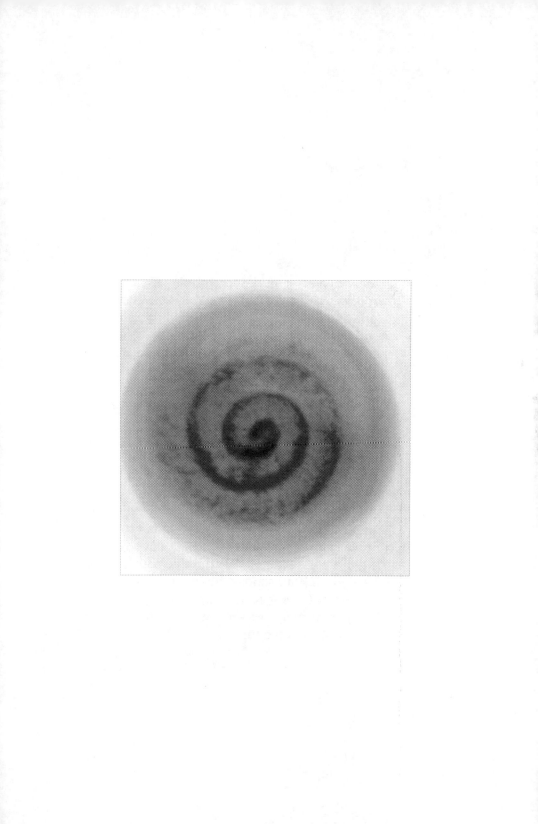

The Rice Is Still Green

At Buddhist memorial ceremonies and funerals, people wear black clothes, eat Buddhist vegetarian food and put their hands together in gasshō, the prayer pose, to symbolize devotion. The word 精進 shōjin can mean 'devotion' or 'Buddhist vegetarian food'. The first character contains the meanings 'blue' and 'rice'. 'Blue' is used in Japanese like 'green' is in English, for vegetables and traffic lights. This means the rice is still green. It is not ripe yet, has not matured enough for harvest. Even if you think the rice is ripe, it is still green inside. You may think you can harvest it, but if you look closely, the grain is not ready. We have to keep devoting ourselves to our path and never think we have mastered something. We should bow down low and become as humble as a rice plant bowing its ear down further as the grain matures. Shōjin food is the most humble food as it avoids killing and self-centered indulgence. Black clothes for mourning are the most humble clothes as they acknowledge our devotion and indebtedness to the deceased. Always remembering our immaturity, we should remain humble.

Taller

Point 30 in Miyamoto Musashi's '35 Strategic Principles' is たけくらべ takekurabe, comparing your height with your partner's. But this is not only a question of physical size. It depends on your mind. If your mind is calm and keeps its focus everywhere, unperturbed by any particular object including your partner, your posture will be good, which changes the way people perceive you, making you look taller than you are. If your mind shrinks, if you get scared or nervous, or worry too much about looking good, you will appear smaller. Be unperturbed and keep good posture at all times.

Undivided Attention

As soon as you think 'Now my technique is good', the fact that you are having this thought means that your thoughts are not fully focused on your technique. You are not giving it your best. And as soon as you think: 'I'm going to do my best', this thought is in the way of doing your best. The double-sided coin of form and mind is a complicated subject. Kaiso Morihei Ueshiba said: 'I am a microcosm of the universe. I am aikido. Aikido is me.' This is perfect harmony between form and mind. As priest of a Zen temple, this would be like saying: 'I am the sutra. The sutra is me.' In aikido, we call this state in which both form and mind harmonize 心身一如 shinshin-ichinyo - 'mind and body as one'. We try to unite mind and body, our partner and ourselves, ourselves and the universe. Striving for this is what we should concentrate on. This is the type of training that allows us to free ourselves from thinking 'Is my form correct' or 'Is my mind correct?' These thoughts interfere with focusing completely on our practice.

One and Zero

One way of thinking is this: your partner attacks with a force of 100, and you add 1. There is no struggle. Strength plus strength is harmony - a kind of harmony in which the partners feel a comfortable pressure, a balanced tension where their bodies touch. The movement feels like a dance involving centrifugal force. Another possibility is this: when you get attacked, make yourself zero. Find the place where you feel zero resistance and, without using force, move that way. Like water that flows naturally into a crevice, fill zero with your existence. In this case, there is no tension between the partners. Uke feels like the partner he attacked has suddenly melted away. Aikido is strength plus strength creating harmony. But aikido is also the courage to make yourself zero. Add your strength up, and the result will be positive. Make yourself zero when you get attacked, and there will be nothing to attack.

Plus, not Minus

Even when facing two much younger, stronger men grabbing me with all their might I can easily make them tumble. Why? Because I am not trying to use my strength against theirs. That would be hopeless. I tore a muscle in my shoulder, so at the moment I cannot lift my arm. In a way, I feel lucky because it reminds me that to do a good technique I do not even need the strength to lift my arm. Partner 1 attacks with 50% strength, partner 2 gives me another 50%. Instead of struggling here and there, trying to take away from their strength and wasting my own, I add 1% of my own power to theirs. Now we have a lot of power combined and can easily achieve a beautiful, effective technique. Aikido is not a minus martial art. It is a plus martial art. There is no fighting involved. True aikido always adds strength to strength, power to power.

如意

Nyoi

What does nyoi mean? Looking at the characters, 如 (nyo) means 'like/as' and 意 (i) means 'intention/will'. So you could interpret this phrase to mean 'As you like it', or 'Do what you want'. But this is not its true meaning. The 意 i refers to Truth, to 佛心 busshin, the Buddha's mind, the Buddha's intentions, and the Buddha's will. So what the phrase really means is that we should always try to live by the Buddha's principles and polish ourselves so we may learn how to express our real nature. We should be conscious and aware of its existence in ourselves and make an effort to practice diligently so we may live to our full potential.

137

而今
Nikon

A lot of people practice aikido with the objective to become a good martial artist or get a black belt. But this is like a shopping trip: you need things, so you make a list. You plan to achieve something in the future. Then you buy everything on the list and take it home. Done. Having a future goal is part of aikido. But in aikido, we are never done. Of course, your techniques will improve, and to achieve this is a good objective. But rather than practicing aikido thinking that one day you will achieve what you are looking for, you should focus on the concept of 而今 nikon. The first character means 'affirmative', 'that', or 'you', the second character means 'now'. Together they constitute an attitude that focuses on the present, the here and now. We should be fully aware of what we are doing and try our very best every moment. If we focus on 而今 nikon, our path will never stop, but we will enjoy the benefits of living with aikido moment by precious moment. Practice here and now. Do your best here and now.

万里一空
Banri
Ikkū

Miyamoto Musashi's school of sword fighting is called 二天一流 niten ichiryū (Two-Heavens-as-One) and uses two swords, one long, one short. After long years of experience, Musashi wrote down 35 Strategic Principles. The last one is 万里一空 banri ikkū, which contains the meaning of them all: 'Everything One Emptiness' or 'All Things One Sky'. We usually try to divide the world into parts and give them names to understand it better. We try to devise rules, principles, and techniques to encounter each situation appropriately. But any 構え kamae (ready stance) that assumes a particular attack is flawed. The perfect kamae is no kamae. Always be ready. For anything. Only once we empty our mind of all preconceptions and expectations can we see things as they are. Make yourself empty and you will see things clearly, moment by moment. According to Musashi, the sword has no mind - it has no special intention, so it can go anywhere, anytime. Remember 万里一空 banri ikkū - Everything One Emptiness. All Things One Sky.

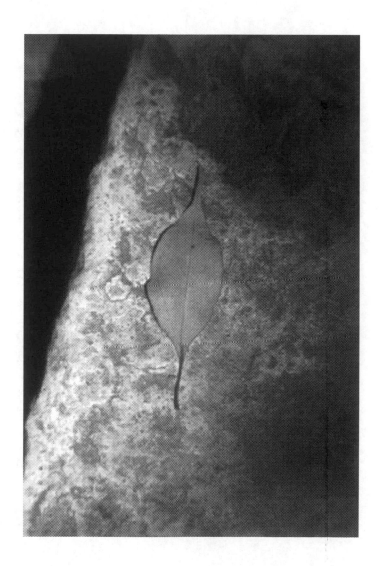

美 Bi – Beauty

In my opinion, 武道 budō (the martial arts) carried to the extreme become a beautiful dance resembling Noh theater. If you practice a martial art diligently and devotedly, your practice will result in 美 bi (beauty). But what is beauty? Ultimately, beauty is anything that gives people joy through sense or mind perception. But practicing with the goal to impress people will warp your efforts. Start on a smaller scale. First, form your own idea of beauty. Try to do things you find beautiful in a way that appears beautiful to you. Express yourself in a way that corresponds with your own idea of beauty. If you keep being strict with yourself as you strive for the achievement of your own, heartfelt idea of beauty, sooner or later, others will begin to see and appreciate the beauty you are working so hard to create. In this way true beauty is born and can be enjoyed by everybody including both creators and witnesses.

The Three Treasures

The three treasures of Buddhism are 仏法僧 buppōsō (仏, Buddha, the one who opened up the path; 法, the content of his teachings; and 僧, those who put his teachings into practice). In aikido, we have our own three treasures. The first treasure is our teacher, by which we refer to O-Sensei who created the path of aikido, and our own teachers passing on the techniques and principles he taught filtered through their efforts and personalities. These teachings constitute the second treasure of aikido. The third treasure are our fellow aikido practitioners who allow us to practice and grow alongside them. Respecting O-Sensei, the creator of aikido is a basic component of choosing this path. Meeting a teacher who can truly inspire us and bring out the best in us is an extremely valuable encounter we should respect and honor with time, effort, and gratefulness. Being able to practice and strive to create harmony with our fellow aikido practitioners is another blessing we must value. Our gratefulness towards others helping us advance on the path should find expression in sincere greetings before and after practice.

An Enlightening Exorcism

One day, a woman came to the temple with her dog. The dog was sick, and she thought his sickness had been brought on by her wearing a fox fur collar. According to her reasoning, foxes belonged to the same family as dogs, so her mindless and cruel fashion purchase had made the dog sick. She regretted having bought the collar and asked me to perform an exorcism on her dog to help him recover. Personally, I found her way of reasoning rather far-fetched, but I respected her feelings, honored her request, and performed the appropriate ceremony. The result was quite surprising. Not only did her dog get better, but another thing happened. Soon after, a whole family of foxes came to live with us here in the grounds of Shosenji Temple. They stuck around for a long time. Friendly, beautiful foxes respectfully sharing our living space with us. For me, this story shows how closely everything in this world is connected. We should remember that we are connected with all sentient beings. If we respect them, we can live harmoniously in their midst.

The Five Teachings

O-Sensei left us five teachings about irimi-nage. When I taught them abroad before without an interpreter, I said O-Sensei had transmitted them to future generations 'mouth to mouth'. I do apologize. The Japanese word 口伝 kuden (oral traditions) written with the characters 'mouth' and 'transmission' made me associate this phrase I had heard somewhere. I simply meant to say they were transmitted by word of mouth rather than written down. **1.** Enter your partner's space. Move into his blind angle. **2.** Keep an iron ring with your arms. This does not mean making them stiff or letting your shoulders get tense. Simply create a circle with your arms, let ki flow through it, and do not let it break throughout your technique. **3.** Return the wave. Create a wave motion. Let the wave rise and return to the shore. **4.** Fold your partner into your sphere of influence. If he is tall, make sure you reduce him to a more compact size, so you can absorb him into your wave and work with him at your own pace. **5.** To finish, point your finger tips down towards the earth and further: towards infinity.

Zanshin 残心 – An Alternative Meaning

Put your shoulder blades together, close to the spine, and down. The very back of your head should point straight up at the sky. For this, pull in your chin a little. Then, your crown can open up and be your connection with the sky. Look at everything at once, let nothing perturb your peace of mind and your good posture. Also, make sure you use 残心 zanshin. Conventionally speaking, zanshin (literally: remaining mind) is interpreted as constant awareness, or the act of looking at your opponent for a little while, maintaining and reinforcing your dominant position after you have fought and won against him. But in aikido, the martial art of peace, it has a different meaning. After you finish a technique, look at your partner and double-check your posture, paying attention to the following points: Did you maintain good posture throughout the technique? Did you succumb to the temptation to fight, become violent, and focus on looking good? Did you bend forward, lose your balance, or tense up? Is your partner safe? Use zanshin in this peaceful, caring sense that promotes self improvement and harmony.

真向法 ......
Makkōhō

Makkōhō is written with the characters 'truth', 'turn towards', and 'method'. The word describes techniques often used in aikido warm-ups that promote good health and posture and guide us towards truth. In Japanese culture, there are two kinds of truth. One refers to factual truth, to 'true' as opposed to 'false'. The other refers to what is right. This truth is equivalent with the mind of the Buddha and our own Buddha nature, our potential to live in harmony with ourselves, others, and the universe. This is the truth we are seeking when we practice makkōhō. Try 振魂の行 furitama no gyō (shaking soul technique) : Lift your arms above your head stretching your body. When your palms meet, turn them so the back of your right hand comes forward and let them drop, left hand on top, across your solar plexus down to your abdomen. Shake them lightly, shoulders relaxed, back straight. This creates waves sending negative energy out, and inviting positive energy in. Try to use this when out of breath. Within seconds your breathing will slow down, and you will feel revitalized. Turn towards truth. Feel the power of makkōhō.

手魂
Tedama

According to Zen master Takuan Soho
(1573-1645), our palms emit a special
type of ki called 生発の気 shōhatsu no
ki (ki that brings forth life). When we
have a headache, we automatically put
a hand on our forehead. When our teeth
hurt, we put a hand on our cheek. We
instinctively know the power emanating
from our palms. Using the power of our
hands to affect our environment is called
手魂 tedama (hand soul). Reacting to
something after it has happened is too
late. Adopt an attitude and demeanor
that does not allow your partner to do
anything you do not want him to do. You
are in control. Things change through
your hands. To let your soul work through
your hands, keep good posture, relax,
breathe calmly, and connect the palms
of your hands seamlessly with your
partner's body. This cannot be achieved
with strength but rather through the
intention to create perfect harmony
and the conscious emission of life
giving ki through your palms.

秋猴の身
Shūkō no Mi –
The Short-Handed
Monkey

We tend to rely on our arms too much. Because we have long arms, we try to stretch them out even further while forgetting about our center, our balance, and the way we shift our body weight, which are all more important than our arms. This is our nature, our weakness. It often means that we use arm strength instead of efficient body movement to execute techniques. Musashi passed on a teaching to us called 秋猴の身 shūkō no mi , the short-handed monkey. The short-handed monkey could do everything just as well as a monkey with long arms by moving his body efficiently. Emulate the short-handed monkey. Now and then, try to do techniques without using your arms, simply by moving well, remaining centered, and keeping your axis stable. This will teach you how to use your body efficiently, and when you add your arms again, things will appear extremely simple and effortless.

Using
A
Weapon

Famous swordsman Miyamoto Musashi said:

'When I have a sword, I don't rely on it,
so not having a sword doesn't faze me.'

If you rely on your sword, it is easy to limit yourself
to whatever techniques are conventionally performed
with a sword. Do not lose your freedom. The best option
might be to throw your sword at your opponent, use your
hands, or employ simple body movement instead of
the sword. Remember you are free. The fact that you
have a sword should afford you the opportunity to use
it, but not take away the opportunity not to use it. Do
not let the sword chop up your world. Let it expand
your reach. Whatever weapon you have, do not let
it limit your mind and body. Maintain freedom of
mind and movement at all times, in all situations.

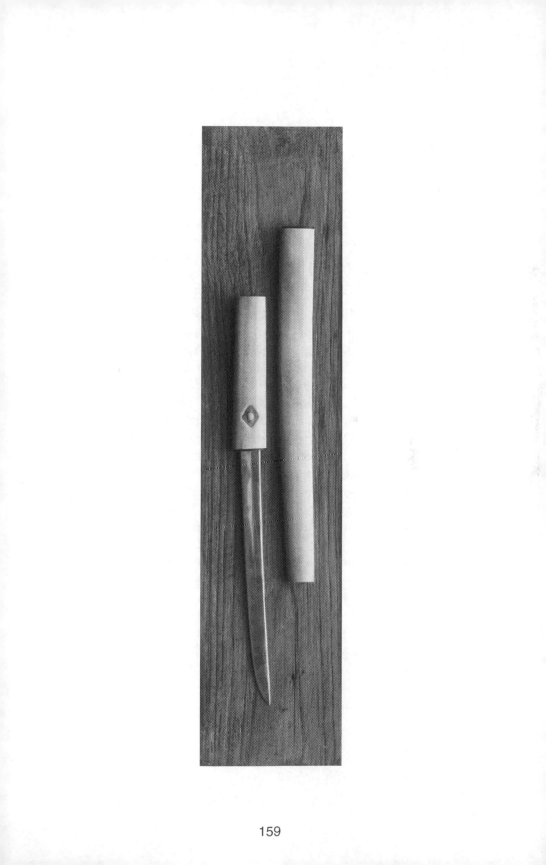

咄嗟 Tossa and 間一髪 Kan Ippatsu

Practicing a technique in a certain way to understand its basics is one type of practice. But after a while, we should proceed to a higher level. We should practice reacting instantaneously and honor each attack with a technique custom tailored to it. Here, the focus shifts from the technical basics to the way we react, which should be 咄嗟 (tossa) - instantaneous. Think of 間一髪 kan ippatsu, written with the characters for 'interval', 'one', and 'hair'. Imagine there is only a hair's width between you and your partner. It is a tiny space, but it is huge compared to your goal. Try to reduce this first to half a hair's width, then to a quarter, and so forth, till you manage to connect seamlessly. But do not push for it. Just perfectly glue yourself to whatever part of himself your partner may offer. Feel for tiny gaps and crevices and gently attach yourself to their bottom line. Attaching yourself will enable you to react more and more promptly, while reacting instantaneously will allow you to attach yourself more and more perfectly. We should keep these helpful concepts in mind.

観箭

Kansen

The word 観箭 kansen is the first thing you see when you enter my dojo. I have engraved it into a wooden plate, carefully distributed dark color to every corner of the characters, let it dry, and placed it above the entrance because I believe it is important to remember this when practicing aikido. 観 kan means 'see', or 'perceive', and 箭 sen means 'arrow'. When you practice aikido, imagine you have an arrow at your throat. This is how strict you should be with yourself - as strict as an arrow pointing at your throat. To others, be kind. This is the mindset you should seek when you enter the dojo. When you practice, imagine you have the point of an arrow at your throat at all times. We are usually very kind to each other when we practice but never forget - we are practicing a martial art, which requires the utmost level of self discipline. You should be focused and alert to the point of 無心 mushin, an empty mind ready for anything at any time, a mind that has grown serene at the point of an arrow.

163

Musashi and the Snake

One day Musashi was meditating next to a monk in the mountains. Both Musashi and the monk were sitting in upright lotus position, breathing calmly. From the outside, they appeared to be doing exactly the same thing. As they sat next to each other in silence, a snake came along. When the snake saw Musashi, it stopped dead in its tracks and pulled back its head in a startled swan neck pose. Even its constantly moving tongue got stuck in its mouth for a second. The snake caught itself, cautiously made a U-turn around Musashi and escaped swiftly across the monk's lap. Even though there seemed to be no difference between Musashi and the monk, the snake could not be fooled. The wild animal clearly felt that Musashi was ready to cut an attacker at any moment. The monk on the other hand, who was doing zazen in the true sense of Zen meditation, was in a state of 空 kū (emptiness). To the snake he was the same as the grass, the stones and the earth it moved across daily, and slithering across his lap did not make the slightest difference.

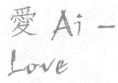

愛 Ai – Love

O-Sensei said the 合 ai in aikido that usually represents the aspect of harmony in the art can also mean 愛 ai - love. Remember this when you practice. There should be no fighting. Resisting the attack does not work. Accepting it does. Disrespecting your partner does not work. Respecting him does. Trying to beat your partner does not work. Holding your partner dear does. When the English word 'love' was first translated into Japanese, its meaning was explained as 'holding somebody or something dear', 'thinking of somebody or something as important'. This is the attitude you should seek when doing aikido. O-Sensei said: 'Do aikido with love.' Otherwise it is not real aikido.

What Goes Around Comes Around

A lot of people pray for world peace, which is very honorable. I believe, however, that rather than praying for world peace, what is even more important is turning ourselves into individuals who can live in peace and create peace around ourselves through our constant efforts in this direction. The same is true for harmony. Instead of praying for harmony, we should nurture love in ourselves and become people who can create harmony. Harmony is the sum of our love. When I was sick, my students formed a circle around me and sent me their ki. Men and women, young and old, short and tall, people of different nationalities and religions, all held each other by the hand. As a result, it became much easier for me to heal. This love and care, this circle of support is true harmony. When I saw such an eclectic circle of people around me, it struck me that harmony is the sum of our love. We need to nurture love and peace in ourselves and send them out into the world.

Let's Dance

If you are strict with yourself and practice hard, your practice will give birth to beauty. Your aikido will turn into a dance. Your movements will come to resemble Noh theater, a traditional Japanese performing art that uses calm, slow, centered movements with good posture, similar to Chinese Tai Chi. Through beauty, through dance, ki can flow smoothly, and you can connect with your center, with others, and with the universe. Let's Dance!

一大事
Ichidaiji

Literally, the characters 一大事 ichi dai ji mean 'one', 'big', and 'thing/issue'. In everyday language, the word is used to refer to a crisis like cancer or a tsunami. In Buddhist terminology the word describes the Buddha's appearance on earth to save all living things. Thinking about the many layers of the word can lead to different interpretations. 一大 for example means 'huge' or 'major'. Followed by 事 (thing/issue) it would mean something like 'a major issue'. 大事 means 'important'. Preceded by 一 (one) it would mean 'the one important thing'. I have only recently managed to gather the essence of this word and reach my own interpretation. The one important thing is being alive here and now. Think of all the effort and love, air, water, energy - all the unlikely factors that had to come together for you to be alive and to be here. Being alive here and now is our greatest treasure. It is the 'major issue', the 'one important thing'. We need to honor each moment of our lives with gratefulness and the most genuine effort to be our best possible selves. This is ichidaiji.

To Do

Pray and promise to
try. Always accept
gratefully. Seek good
form and good attitude.
Be yourself and respect
others. Practice hard
and give birth to beauty.
Dance. Take each fall
gratefully as an opportunity
to practice getting up. Sit
and be silent. Connect
with yourself, with others,
and with the world.
Create harmony.

Aikido Glossary

aemono	和え物	'harmonious thing' - a Japanese type of dish that combines two or more ingredients so their flavors complement each other perfectly
ai	合	harmony/encounter/interaction
ai	愛	love
aiki	合気	the principle of harmony
banri ikkū	万里一空	'Everything One Emptiness' or 'All Things One Sky' - Point 35 in Musashi's 35 Strategic Principles
bi	美	beauty
budō	武道	the martial arts
buppōsō	仏法僧	the three treasures of Buddhism: Buddha; his teachings; and those practicing his Way
busshin	佛心	the mind of the Buddha
dan	段	grading system used in aikido and many other Japanese disciplines for higher grades starting from shodan (first black belt) and going up to jūdan (10th dan). The 10th dan is rarely awarded and based not on a particular test but on formidable skill and personality, and services performed in the aikido world. Only about 10 people have ever been awarded 10th dan, some of them, including Shimamoto Shihan's teacher Kisaburo Osawa, posthumously.
dango	団子	sweet, sticky Japanese rice balls
-dō	-道	affix for Japanese systems of self-improvement
fudōshin	不動心	the immovable mind/ Zen mind
funiki	雰囲気	atmosphere

furitama no gyō	振魂の行	'shaking soul' technique taken from makkōhō - left palm on right, shake hands in front of the abdomen to release negative and invite positive energy
gaiki	外気	'external ki' - the ki we send out
gansei	願誓	the two aspects of prayer: request and pledge
gasshō	合掌	hand gesture used for prayer, expressing gratitude, humility, and devotion: hands together in front of the chest or nose
hakama	袴	black skirt-like wrap-around pants worn over the dogi by higher grades in aikido (the details vary according to dojos and organizations - at Shosenji - aikikai affiliated- women wear hakama from 3rd kyu, men from first dan). Originally Intended to hide footwork from potential opponents and copycats.
heijōshin	平常心	in everyday language: unperturbed mind. Shimamoto Shihan explaining the Buddhist meaning of the term: 'Our constant diligent effort to be our best possible selves.'
hōshin	放心	disengaging the mind
ichidaiji	一大事	in everyday language: a serious problem. Shimamoto Shihan: 'The fact that we are alive here and now. Honor it.'
ichimizen	一未禅	applying the Zen mind to everything in life
in	印	mudra - hand gesture
irimi-nage	入り身投げ	'entering throw' - a technique in which the partner is thrown by entering, sweeping him up and guiding him down
Kaiso	開祖	refers to aikido founder Morihei Ueshiba (1883-1969), also frequently called ' O-Sensei'

kamae	構え	ready stance - pose/ attitude adopted in order to get ready for a certain attack or other occurrence
kan	観	a sixth sense, heightened sensibility
kan ippatsu	間一髪	a hair's width
kansen	観箭	imagining an arrow at one's throat
katame	固め	pin - a type of move designed to hold one's partner in place, performed at the end of many aikido techniques
keiko	稽古	practice - word used for practicing traditional methods of self improvement
ken	見	eyesight
ken no me yowaku, kan no me tsuyoku	見の目弱く、観の目強く	saying by Miyamoto Musashi meaning that intuition is more reliable than eyesight
ki	気	vital energy. Mind waves. Shimamoto Shihan: 'Prayer.' The power we seek to cultivate and learn to direct in aikido.
ki no nagare	気の流れ	the flow of ki
kū	空	emptiness
kuden	口伝	traditions transmitted only by word of mouth
kyū	級	grading system used in aikido and other Japanese disciplines for lower grades. Details vary according to dojos and organizations. At Shosenji there are 5 kyū grades. Junior grades wear colored belts matching their kyū. Adults sometimes wear a brown belt from 3rd, 2nd, or 1st kyū.
maai	間合い	distance, angles, and spacing in a martial encounter

makkōhō	真向法	Japanese techniques aimed at better flexibility and mind/body balance
michi	道	path
Miyamoto Musashi	宮本武蔵	famous Japanese swordsman (1584-1645) who wrote the '35 Strategic Principles' and later the famous 'Book of Five Rings' based on this text
mizu no kokoro	水の心	'mind of water' - a completely calm mind able to perceive reality as it is
mushin	無心	an empty state of mind (also see fudōshin)
naiki	内気	'internal ki' - the ki inside ourselves/used for ourselves
nikon	而今	living here and now
niten ichiryū	二天一流	'Two-Heavens-as-One' - Miyamoto Musashi's sword fighting school that employs two swords
noh	能	a traditional Japanese theater form that involves elaborate masks and costumes, rhythm, music, singing, and dancing in very slow, stylized, controlled movements
nyoi	如意	following the Buddha's will
omoiyari	思いやり	consideration for others
omote-waza	表技	forward techniques
O-Sensei	大先生	refers to aikido founder Morihei Ueshiba (1883-1969), also frequently called 'Kaiso' in Japanese
sakura dango	桜団子	a green, a pink, and a white sticky rice ball on a skewer - eaten especially during cherry blossom season

shikantaza	只管打坐	Soto Zen teaching: practice zazen; sit only in order to sit
shinshinichinyo	心身一如	mind and body as one
shizentai	自然体	literally 'natural body' or 'natural posture' - being and acting without pretense. Shimamoto Shihan's interpretation: straight back, shoulder blades together and down, shoulders relaxed, wide field of vision, breathing relaxed, mind relaxed, ki relaxed, knees relaxed and ready to move
shōjin	精進	devotion; Buddhist vegetarian food
sottaku dōji	啐啄同時	the joint effort of hen and chick to make the chick burst out of the egg
shūkō no mi	秋猴の身	the short-handed monkey - a concept used by Miyamoto Musashi to explain that efficient body movement is crucial
takekurabe	たけくらべ	Point 30 in Musashi's 35 Strategic Principles: comparing your height with your partner's
tedama	手魂	'hand soul' - influencing the outcome of things
tenchi-nage	天地投げ	'heaven-earth throw' - an aikido technique in which the partner is thrown by pointing one hand up at the sky and the other down at the earth
tenchijin	天地人	Heaven-Earth-Man
tori	取り	the person executing the technique in aikido
tossa	咄嗟	instantaneous
uchi-mizu	打ち水	Japanese custom of sprinkling water in the entrance hall before a guest arrives
uke	受け	the person attacking and taking falls in aikido

urawaza	裏技	backward techniques
wa	和	harmony/plus
wafudō	和不同	harmony does not equal sameness
wagō	和合	harmony
yakuza	ヤクザ	Japanese mafia
yasashisa	優しさ	kindness
yūkō mukō	有構無構	kamae is no kamae
zazen	坐禅	seated meditation
zanshin	残心	remaining mind

ZEN

Aikido and Zen

The word 一如 ichinyo consists of the characters for 'one' and 'like'. This is how the relationship between aikido and Zen can be described. Of course the two are separate disciplines. They each have their own history and form. They are not the same. But in essence, they are like one. The attitude we seek and the truth we try to experience and integrate into our dealings with the world are the same in Zen and aikido. This is why the following pages are dedicated to communicating some of the basic building blocks of Zen that may be useful to the aikido practitioner and anybody else enjoying this book.

What is Zen?

Zen is a Japanese form of Buddhism. In Sanskrit, the word for Zen is 'zenna'. The Japanese character 禅 Zen was chosen to represent its sound. Its meaning has been translated into Japanese as 定 jō (Sanskrit: samadhi - a state in which the mind becomes one with the experienced object and exists in complete serenity), 静慮 jōryo (Sanskrit: dhyana - a meditative state of deep concentration), and 思惟修 shiyuishu (calm, even thoughts). All these words express the idea that the true nature of things can be recognized by human beings in spite of the attachment and desire that ties them to the duality of the world, and that mind and body can manifest this realization. To achieve this, the mind needs to be perfectly focused, yet all inclusive. As long as you only look at the surface of things and preoccupy yourself with their form, as long as you have likes and dislikes and distinguish between good and bad, you cannot reach this state. Overcoming distraction and duality and becoming one with the Buddha nature in us is also called 解脱 gedatsu, or Nirvana (the character in the image, 佛 hotoke, signifies 'Buddha'). The true meaning of Zen is to inhabit this state with both mind and body.

Heart-to-Heart Zen

The Soto school of Zen believes in 教外別伝 kyōgebetsuden (special transmissions outside the scriptures), 不立文字 furyūmonji (no dependence on words or letters), and 以心伝心 isshindenshin (non-verbal heart-to-heart, mind-to-mind communication), meaning that the true heart of Zen cannot be understood relying on scriptures or oral explanations. The idea is to transmit it in a more direct way. It has to be experienced rather than learned intellectually. A vital message we can send to others to communicate with them from heart to heart is a sincere greeting. Fill each greeting with genuine respect, gratefulness, humility, and appreciation. This is heart-to-heart communication in its purest form.

Focusing Genuinely on No Purpose

When you do zazen, simply sit. Do not think about relieving stress, becoming a great fighter, or attaining enlightenment. Do not think about anything. Simply sit. Only then will you be able to experience fudōshin, mushin, or kū. True emptiness cannot contain a purpose. Emptiness of mind can also be achieved in everyday activities. At Zen monasteries, 作務 samu (manual labor such as cleaning and gardening) is part of the monks' daily schedule. Watch a chef peel potatoes. He does this every day. The knife sits snug in his hand, moves swiftly and smoothly. He has perfected the art of peeling potatoes so much, he can think of absolutely nothing, yet his hands keep peeling in a perfect, efficient, beautiful way. Genuinely focusing all his attention on one activity, he is able to attain a state of mushin (no mind). Try to find activities in your daily life you can focus on so genuinely that you become one with the activity, allowing your mind to become empty. The important part is that you focus on the activity itself, not on its outcome. You clean, for example, not because you want a clean house. Instead, you dedicate yourself fully to the process. Clean!

只管打坐
Shikantaza

If the surface of a lake is completely still, the moon appears in it without the slightest distortion. If there is a half moon, the water reflects a perfect half moon. If there is a sickle moon, the water reflects a perfect sickle moon. We call this 水の心 mizu no kokoro (mind of water).

While this concept does express a Zen ideal, you should have no objective in mind when you devote yourself to zazen. Simply sit and do your best at all times without comparing yourself to others. You are the universe. Simply sit. Breathe calmly, keep good posture, and let your thoughts flow by.

This individual devotion to zazen, the simple act of focusing 100% on sitting, is called 只管打坐 shikantaza, which constitutes the central pillar of Soto Zen. Simply sit, being your best possible self.

Zen Evolution

In Zen, there are five stages of development.

The first stage is 外道禅 gedōzen. You are simply living your life without a set perspective. You are experiencing the world outside the Way.

The second stage is 凡夫 bonpu. You have understood that the world is ungraspable and entered the Way. We have this sensation in the dark, when we cannot see what is what. You have understood emptiness.

The third stage is 小乗禅 shōjōzen. You have grasped the logic of life: when you do something good, something good will come back. Whatever energy you send out will return. You efforts are focused on yourself. You polish your personality and purify your spirit.

The fourth stage is 大乗禅 daijōzen. You extend your efforts to creating harmony with others. You become part of a communal effort towards peace.

The final stage is 最大乗禅 saidaijōzen. You have returned to your original self. We call this 新起源 shinkigen, or 'new beginning'. You have returned to 自性 jishō, your Buddha nature. Your mind has become serene. A new beginning. A clean slate.

印 In – Hand Gestures

印 In are hand gestures derived from ancient Indian traditions. In English, the Sanskrit term 'mudra' is more common. In are used in many spiritual, physical, and artistic disciplines including Hinduism, Buddhism, Taoism, yoga, Indian dance, and Asian martial arts. Their purpose ranges from health promotion to spiritual and religious symbolism, greeting, prayer, esoteric and magical practices.

In yoga, in are used to assist practitioners with specific breathing exercises. In Buddhist iconography, they are associated with concepts like 'protection' or 'knowledge', or with certain representations of the Buddha. Religious sects like Shingon Buddhism use them for esoteric practices. Martial arts like kung fu and ninjutsu use them to focus the mind, strengthen the body, and assist practitioners on dangerous and difficult missions.

It has been found that in stimulate the mind in the same way as language does. They are physical manifestations of human spirit, a physical attempt to communicate more deeply with others, with the guiding powers on our spiritual path, and with the universe. In are aimed at expressing and enacting a human ideal the practitioner strives for, and at seeking a connection with the sources that can guide him towards his goal.

Zazen

Zazen is a type of seated meditation. Siddhartha Gautama Buddha, called 'Shaka', 'O-Shaka-san', or 'Shakuson' in Japanese was enlightened after meditating under the Bodhi tree. As he used seated meditation to become enlightened, many schools of Buddhism place great emphasis on the use of zazen. In Soto Zen, zazen is considered the most important part of the practitioner's spiritual life, practiced in meditation sessions called 坐禅会 zazenkai. Practicing zazen is often associated with enlightenment, dissolving duality, freeing oneself of desire, and becoming one with the Buddha nature that lies hidden in each of us. The main characteristic of Soto Zen, however, is its teaching that there is no objective to zazen. The meaning of zazen according to Soto Zen is to sit simply in order to sit (只管打坐 shikantaza). In the following, you will find an explanation of the etiquette and form used at a Soto zazenkai. Please note that this is only one way of practicing zazen. Every temple may have its own rules, and the specific meditation protocol may vary. Please follow the rules that apply wherever you choose to practice.

Before the Zazenkai

Take off your watch, accessories, and shoes. Enter the meditation hall (zendō) with your hands in shashu,[1] stepping in with your left foot on the left side of the entrance. With your hands in gasshō,[2] bow towards the altar and go to your spot. When walking, keep your hands in shashu. Refrain from talking inside the zendō. Do not cross in front of the Buddha statue but walk around it. Use a meditation cushion (zafu) that has the right shape and size for your body. When sitting down, make sure you line up properly with the people next to you. Once the zazen practitioners have taken their positions, the supervisor of the zazenkai enters, makes his rounds in the zendō, and examines whether everybody is sitting correctly. This is called 検単 kentan. When the supervisor is right behind you, unite your hands in gasshō. When he has passed, return them to hokkaijōin.[3] To signal the start of the zazenkai, a bell is rung three times. This is called shijōshō. After the bell has been rung nobody can enter or leave the zendō until the zazenkai is over.

---

[1] shashu 叉手 - for standing or walking: left thumb in the center of the palm, fingers wrapped around it; left hand in front of the solar plexus, right hand wrapped around it
[2] gasshō 合掌 - prayer pose: hands together in front of the chest or nose
[3] hokkaijōin 法界定印 - used in zazen: left hand on right, palms up, thumbs touching

合掌
Gasshō

This in stands for prayer. It expresses
respect, faith and devotion. The two
hands represent duality. Bringing them
together is a a symbol of the One Mind,
the Buddha mind, or the mind of the
cosmos we belong to. It also represents
the request and the pledge we make
when we pray, asking an external power
for help while promising that we will
contribute as much as we can to the
outcome we hope for. Hold the palms
and fingers of both hands together,
pointing straight up. Your fingertips
should be either at the same height
as your nose, or in front of your chest
bone, and about 4 inches away from
your body. There should be a slight
tension in your elbows, while your
shoulders remain relaxed. Keep
your back straight at all times.

叉手
Shashu

This is the hand gesture
used for walking meditation
(hokōzen/kinhin) or while
standing or walking in the
zendō. Fold the thumb of
your left hand inwards onto
your palm. Wrap your fingers
around it. Place your left
hand in front of your solar
plexus, palm facing your body.
Wrap your right hand around it.
Form a straight line with your
forearms, elbows protruding
left and right of your body.
Relax your shoulders and let
ki flow through your hands,
so you can feel a connection
of slight mutual pressure
between them.

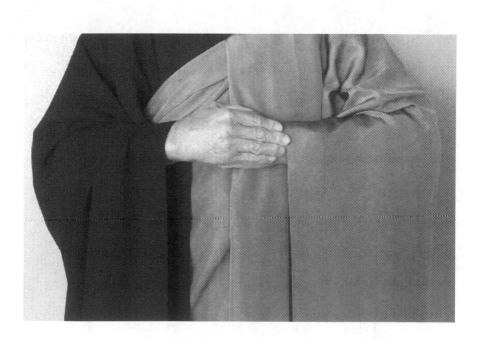

法界定印

Hokkaijōin -
'The Cosmic
Mudra'

This is the in used for sitting in the lotus position or in 正座 seiza[1]. Hands rest in your lap, palms up, fingertips facing. Slide your left hand onto your right. Your thumbs meet and form a circle. Let the tips of your thumbs touch lightly. Do not use strength or push, but never let them come apart.

---

[1]seiza 正座 - Japanese formal kneeling position: thighs on calves, buttocks on the back of the feet, straight back

隣位問訊
Rinimonjin

対坐問訊
Taizamonjin

隣位問訊 Rinimonjin - Greeting
the Zen Practitioners Next to You

Greet the people to your left and
right. When you arrive where you
will sit down for your meditation,
turn to your neighbor and bow
with your hands in gasshō[1] Then
bow to your other neighbor. They
will return the same greeting.

対坐問訊 Taizamonjin - Greeting
the Zen Practitioners Opposite You

Greet the people opposite you.
After you have greeted the people
beside you, keep your hands in
gasshō and bow to the people on
the other side of the zendō. They
will return the same greeting.

---

[1] gasshō 合掌 - prayer pose: hands together in front
of the chest or nose

警策 kyōsaku – A Striking Tool

警策 kyōsaku is short for 警覚策励 keikaku sakurei, meaning 'attention booster'. The kyōsaku is a 2 ft staff used to hit zazen practitioners when they need help staying focused. If a practitioner feels himself getting sleepy, or notices that his attention is waning during zazen, he can unite his hands in gasshō and ask to be hit with the kyōsaku. If the person supervising the zazenkai sees that a practitioner has bad posture or has fallen asleep, he can take the initiative and hit him with the kyōsaku. In both cases, the right shoulder is touched lightly to warn the Zen practitioner of the pending strike. The practitioner then tilts his head to the left to open access to his shoulder. After being hit, he leaves his hands in gasshō and bows before returning them to hokkaijōin[1].

---

[1] hokkaijōin 法界定印/cosmic mudra - hand gesture used in zazen: left hand on right, palms up, thumbs touching

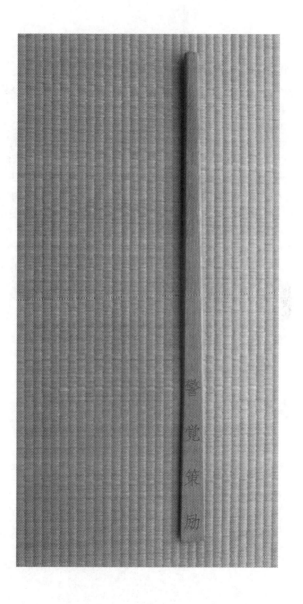

坐蒲 — Zafu

The zafu is a thick, round cushion meant to function as a wedge between your body and the floor that allows your spine to remain straight, while your knees touch the floor throughout the session. Before you sit down, put its edge on the tatami and turn it around, squeezing it lightly, fixing its shape. After the session, return it to its original shape and position in the same way. On one side it has a white tag, which serves as a name tag for zazen practitioners at this temple, so it could carry somebody's name. Proper zazen etiquette requires to bring your own zafu. When you finalize the position of your zafu, the tag should be in the middle, facing away from you.

面壁 Menpeki — Facing the Wall

Turn towards the wall. After you have greeted the people next to you and the people on the other side of the room, sit down on your zafu. Place the center of the zafu under your spine. Push the tatami with one hand and turn towards the wall.

結跏趺坐 Kekkafuza – The Lotus Position

Put your right foot on your left thigh, as close to your pelvic bone as possible. Then, place your left foot on your right thigh, again, as close to your pelvic bone as possible. Your knees should touch the floor. After crossing your legs, form hokkaijōin[1] with your hands and rest them in your lap under your navel.

半跏趺坐 Hankafuza – The Half Lotus Position

For the half lotus position, only the left foot is placed on the right thigh as close to the pelvic bone as possible, while the right foot remains on the ground. What is important in both kekkafuza and hankafuza is that both knees are touching the floor, and a stable triangle is formed between the buttocks and the two knees to support the body.

---

[1] hokkaijōin 法界定印/cosmic mudra - hand gesture used in zazen: left hand on right, palms up, thumbs touching

Upper Body

Your spine should be straight, your lower abdomen pushed forward, stabilizing your pelvis. Relax both shoulders, pull back your chin without putting any strain on your neck, and open the top of your head towards the sky.

Eyes

Do not close your eyes. Keep them naturally open and cast them downwards at a 45 degree angle, looking at a spot about 3 ft in front of you on the floor. Do not let your eyes wander. Keep your focus on this spot.

Mouth

Close your mouth. Imagine your palate near your eyes. With your tongue, touch your upper front teeth as if pronouncing an 'L'. Leave your mouth in this position and do not open or move it during the zazenkai.

欠気一息 Kankiissoku – Exhale Completely

After taking on the right position for zazen, take a deep breath in through your nose, and breathe out gradually through your mouth until all air has left your lungs. After taking a few deep breaths and exhaling through your mouth in this fashion, return to a natural way of breathing through your nose.

覚触 Kakusoku – Awareness

Let your thoughts flow by like a river. Try not to let them catch anywhere and progress logically or associatively. Try not to get emotionally involved. Simply observe them like something outside of you. Do not get involved in the pictures that appear in front of your eyes, the sounds that hit your ears, the smells that invade your nose, or the ideas that emerge in your mind. Neither pursue nor escape them. Allow them to enter and pass freely. The most important thing in zazen is to awaken (kakusoku) from distraction (thinking) or dullness (drowsiness) and return to the right posture moment by moment. As your breathing becomes calm, so does your mind. Do not let anything distract you.

経行 Kinhin/ 歩行禅 Hokōzen— Walking Meditation

Kinhin/ hokōzen is a type of walking meditation performed after practicing zazen. When the bell is rung twice during a zazenkai, this signals the beginning of kinhin. Unite your hands in gasshō, rock your body left and right, unfold your legs, turn right, and stand up. Put your zafu back in place. Bow to your neighbors and the people opposite you. Form shashu[1] with your hands. Starting with your right foot, advance half a foot's length between each inhale and exhale, quietly lifting the heel of the back foot before you place it in front of the other. Do not stomp or lift your feet. Keep them on the ground, slowly sliding forward. Advance clockwise around the zendō and maintain the same distance between you and your neighbors. Pay attention to your breath and posture. Keep eyes and mouth as in zazen. When the bell is rung once put your feet together and stop. Bow. Continuing in the same direction walk back to your spot at a normal pace. Bow to your neighbors and the people opposite you and return to zazen.

---

[1]shashu 叉手 - left thumb in the center of the palm, fingers wrapped around it; left hand in front of the solar plexus, right hand wrapped around it

The Bell

To indicate the start of the zazenkai a bell is rung three times. This is called shijōshō. To indicate the beginning of kinhin,[1] the bell is rung twice. This is called kinhinshō. To signal the end of the walking meditation, the bell is rung once, which is called chūkaishō. To end the entire zazenkai, the bell is again rung once, which is called hōzenshō.

左右揺振 Sayūyōshin – Rocking

This is done to ease the body into the meditating position before zazen, and again to ease it back into unfolding the legs and standing up afterwards. Before you start meditating, rock your body left and right like a pendulum, starting with large movements, then letting them get smaller and smaller, until you have aligned belly button and nose and settled in a stable position in the center. Straighten your back, put your shoulder blades together and down. Your crown should be open to the sky.

---

[1] kinhin 経行/hokōzen 歩行禅 - walking meditation

The End of the Zazenkai

When the bell is rung once, it indicates the end of the zazenkai. Unite your hands in gasshō and bow. Then, place them on your knees palms up and, this time starting with the opposite side, rock your body left and right in increasingly bigger movements. When you are ready, unfold your legs, and face right. Kneel with the balls of your feet supporting your weight, return your zafu to the right shape and position, and stand up. Bow to your neighbors and the people opposite you and leave the zendō with your hands in shashu.[1]

---

[1] shashu 叉手 - hand gesture used in the zendō when standing or walking: left thumb in the center of the palm, fingers wrapped around it; left hand palm down in front of the solarplexus, right hand wrapped around it from above

Zen Glossary

bonpu	凡夫	second stage of spiritual development in Zen
chūkaishō	抽解鐘	bell rung once to indicate the end of kinhin/hokōzen
cosmic mudra/ hokkaijōin	法界定印	hand gesture used in zazen: left hand on right, palms up, thumbs touching
daijōzen	大乗禅	fourth stage of spiritual development in Zen
dhyana / jōryo	静慮	alternative term for 'Zen': state of deep concentration
fudōshin	不動心	'the immovable mind'/ Zen mind
furyūmonji	不立文字	Soto Zen teaching: things are not built on letters
gasshō	合掌	hand gesture used for prayer, expressing gratitude, humility, and devotion: hands together in front of the chest or nose
gedatsu	解脱	nirvana, complete detachment from desire and duality
gedōzen	外道禅	lowest/first stage of spiritual development in Zen
hankafuza	半跏趺坐	half lotus position: left foot on right thigh
hokkaijōin	法界定印	cosmic mudra - hand gesture used in zazen: left hand on right, palms up, thumbs touching
hokōzen	歩行禅	walking meditation (also see: kinhin 経行)
hōzensho	放禅鐘	bell rung once to indicate the end of the zazenkai
ichinyō	一如	like one
in	印	hand gesture/mudra

isshindenshin	以心伝心	Soto Zen teaching: heart-to-heart communication
jishō	自性	original Buddha nature that exists in each human being
jō	定	samadhi - alternative term for 'Zen': serene state of mind
jōryo	静慮	dhyana - alternative term for 'Zen': state of deep concentration
kakusoku	覚触	awareness
kankiissoku	欠気一息	breathing method used initially during zazen: exhale completely before breathing in
kentan	検単	checking the zazen practioners' posture before the zazenkai starts
kekkafuza	結跏趺坐	lotus position: right foot on left thigh, left foot on right thigh
kinhin	経行	walking meditation (also see hokōzen)
kinhinshō	経行鐘	bell rung twice to indicate the beginning of kinhin/hokōzen
kū	空	emptiness
kyōgebetsuden	教外別伝	Soto Zen teaching: outside the teachings, separate from the traditions
kyōsaku	警策	2 ft staff used to hit zazen practitioners and help them focus
menpeki	面壁	facing the wall for zazen
mushin	無心	'no mind' - an ultimately calm state of mind
O-Shaka-san	お釈迦さん	'Buddha' in Japanese
rinimonjin	隣位問訊	bowing to the zazen practitioners next to you

saidaijōzen	最大乗禅	highest/fifth stage of spiritual development in Zen
samu	作務	manual labor Zen monks engage in as part of their spiritual practice
seiza	正座	Japanese formal kneeling position: thighs on calves, buttocks on the back of the feet, back straight
sayūyōshin	左右揺振	rocking the body left and right before and after zazen
shaka	釈迦	'Buddha' in Japanese
shakuson	釈尊	'Buddha' in Japanese
shashu	叉手	hand gesture used in the zendō when standing or walking, and for hokōzen/kinhin: left thumb in the center of the palm, fingers wrapped around it; left hand in front of the solar plexus, right hand wrapped around it from above
shijōshō	止静鐘	bell rung three times as a signal to start the zazenkai
shikantaza	只管打坐	Soto Zen teaching: practice zazen; sit only in order to sit
shinkigen	新起源	'new beginning' - return to one's Buddha nature
shiyuishu	思惟修	alternative term for 'Zen': calm, even thoughts
shōjōzen	小乗禅	third stage of spiritual development in Zen
tatami	畳	straw mat used for flooring in traditional Japanese houses and temples
taizamonjin	対坐問訊	bowing to the zazen practitioners opposite you
zafu	坐蒲	thick round cushion used as a wedge between buttocks and tatami during zazen

Zen	禅	a Japanese form of Buddhism
zazen	坐禅	seated meditation
zazenkai	坐禅会	a Zen meditation session
zendō	禅堂	meditation room

Anna Sanner,
Author

Anna Sanner, born 1980 in Hannover, Germany, holds an MA in Interpreting & Translating Japanese. She has lived in Germany, Canada, the UK, Spain, Japan, and Hawaii and worked as a script writer, director, language teacher, interpreter, translator, and show ninja. Her martial arts background is in karate and aikido. In Osaka, she studied aikido under Zen priest and aikido 8th dan Katsuyuki Shimamoto. She began taking notes on his teachings the first day she met him and has since accompanied him on numerous teaching trips to Canada, Belgium, Poland, Israel, and the Netherlands, serving as his interpreter at aikido and Zen seminars. Since 2010 she has published several aikido related articles in Aikido Journal. More of her writing can be found at:

http://aksanner.blogspot.com
http://kunoichihe.blogspot.com
www.headspace.jp
http://mahaloworld.blogspot.com

Morteza Ariana, Photographer & Designer

Morteza Ariana is a professional photographer and graphic designer. Born in Tehran in 1964, he later left Iran and moved to Germany, where he worked as a freelance photographer. This led him to Malawi, Mozambique, Southeast Asia, and Korea. He also traveled extensively through South America, photographing people in the context of their daily lives. In 2001 he moved to Japan. He incorporates Zen art and wabi-sabi influences into his photography, resulting in several exhibitions in Osaka and Kobe. Since 2009 he has deepened his connection with East Asian arts as an art dealer with the goal of introducing talented young artists from East Asia to the Western markets.